"WE CAN TAKE IT"

BY
RAY HOYT

"WE CAN TAKE IT"

A Short Story of the C.C.C.

BY

RAY HOYT

With Illustrations by
MARSHALL DAVIS

AMERICAN BOOK COMPANY

New York   Cincinnati   Chicago
Boston   Atlanta

AN UNCOMMON VALOR REPRINT EDITION
Complete and Unabridged

Printed in the United States of America

ISBN: 979-8869082008

PREFACE

IT IS not difficult to write of such physical things as fire breaks, barracks, Army officers, millions of dollars, or hundreds of thousands of men. It is easy to tell, page by page, about miles of roads built, acres of land cleared, and dams erected against soil erosion. It is but a simple task of reporting to repeat what others have said about them. But when one deals with matters not so tangible, one attempts a far more difficult and more important work than that of a mere recorder. The real nature of the Civilian Conservation Corps, or rather the spirit which pervades its ranks, is such an incorporeal thing.

The trails which the men of the C.C.C. have built through the forests of the nation during the past two years, the timber lands they have cleared of snags and underbrush and insect pests, are monuments to a new type of forest worker. Earlier trails had been built and other lands had been cleared of fire hazards by men to whom the labor was nothing but toil, at so much per hour. But there has been something personal in the work of the C.C.C. men; something of themselves has been laid down with each mile of new road and each acre of timber saved from fire or blight.

There has grown up among the men of this new forest army from the towns and cities a spirit that is new. It is a new kind of patriotism: not one drummed up through emotions, but one that springs from the soil. It is a patriotism that involves trees and hillsides and streams, and is fused with one's interest in one's family and one's own future, and, too, one's feeling of gratitude toward a government that has given rather than taken away.

To these C.C.C. men, benefits from government are not merely such obscure advantages as the protection of property or the saving of the individual from exploitation or death by acts of those who are stronger or who have heavier weapons. To these C.C.C. men the incorporeal benefit is something quite as real as a job of physical work at a time when there are few jobs to be had. They recognize the reality of this, and it makes them thankful to their government and ties them closer to it. A patriotism that grows from an understanding of the powers of nature and the interest of the government in one's own future is a potent force. It is in such patriotism that the Spirit of the C.C.C. is rooted.

The writer has had the opportunity of being with the men in camp, of eating at their mess tables, of reading thousands of letters describing their work and their play and their reactions to camp life, to their officers, and to the forests and parks, and their thoughts about their families at home and about their government. It is easy to write of the forests and the men, but difficult to picture such intangibles as this Spirit of the C.C.C. It is hoped, however, that this short story of the C.C.C. and Emergency Conservation Work at least will call general attention to a nation's great attempt to conserve the "national resources" of the country; to the thousands of young men who are participating in this gigantic "experiment" in natural and human conservation and rehabilitation; and to the new patriotism that has sprung from their contact with nature, government, and the need of a job.

R. H.

CONTENTS

ILLUSTRATIONS

WHERE DO WE GO FROM HERE? 6

*** 1 ***

A NEW DEAL FOR YOUTH

ON MARCH 4, 1933, a new President was inaugurated On March 9 a new Congress met, and on the same day a group of seven men, including the President, held an important meeting in the White House.

The new President had been elected in November. Things had not been going well with the country, and, in the preceding campaign, he had said much about the existing widespread unemployment and about "the forgotten man." He had proposed a "new deal." He had mentioned conservation of natural resources as a part of it. And the voters had decided that some sort of "new deal" might help things.

It was at the White House, March 9, between four o'clock in the afternoon and ten o'clock at night, that the Civilian Conservation Corps was given its swaddling clothes and began its toddling steps, — the infant that has grown so soon into the ruddy-faced, hard-muscled giant of today. Seated around the President's desk, the other six men, who had come hurriedly at his request, listened as he talked about trees and men. He was a lover of trees. He talked of their importance to a country. He also talked of the importance of young men to the life and future of a nation. He had a plan for the saving of growing trees and of young men. That was the beginning of the C.C.C.

The Secretary of War was there; so were the Secretary of Agriculture and the Secretary of the Interior. The others present were the Director of the Budget, the Solicitor of the Department of the Interior, and the Judge Advocate General of the Army. For two hours this group listened as the Presi-

7

dent talked about forests struggling to survive the ravages of carelessness and greed. That struggle was a losing battle for the forests. The President knew much about reforestation. It had been close to his heart for many years. He knew about watersheds that had been denuded of growth and had become breeding grounds for destructive floods. He believed in the necessity of protecting the wooded regions of the country against fire hazards. He envisaged a reclamation and conservation program that would cover the entire country.

The President talked also about the young men of the country who needed a "break." There were 5,000,000 or more of them between the ages of 18 and 25 years who had come into man's estate, ready to go to work, but who could find no work to do. Some had had jobs, but had been forced out by the economic depression. Others had left school for the same reason. Most of them never had had a job. All were of the age when lack of something around which to wrap their minds and hands might prove disastrous for them, and for the country of which they formed so large a part. Conservation of these human resources was much more important even than the saving of natural resources.

The plan which the President outlined involved both forests and young men. It would place as many young men as possible at work in the forests and along the streams. The men would be picked from cities, towns, and farms, and transported into the woods. There they would live and work, planting trees, reducing hazards of forest fires, clearing streams, and checking destruction caused by soil erosion.

This meeting was not a conference. The new President asked few questions of the men he had called before him. He talked. He laid his plan before them. He wanted half a million young men placed at work; or, if enough funds were not available for so many, then as large a number as possible. But he wanted it done immediately. That was the reason for the meeting. The Department of Agriculture and the Department of the Interior are charged with the control of national forests and national parks. The Department of War was the only government agency so organized that it could, on short notice, enroll, clothe, and feed several hundred thousand men and supervise them in work camps. The project would cost money. That was why the Director of the Budget was there. There were legal aspects to consider, and a bill to be drafted for presentation to Congress. That accounted for the presence of the Judge Advocate General of the Army and the Solicitor of the Department of the Interior.

Was the idea a good one? the President asked. All six men agreed that it was. Could the plan be set in motion immediately? The Secretary of War said it could. Was there work in the forests and parks of the country that these men might do? The Secretary of Agriculture and the Secretary of the Interior were certain of it. Could the idea be put at once into the necessary legal form for presentation to Congress? The Judge Advocate General assured the President that it could be done.

"Can it all be ready by nine o'clock tonight?" the President asked.

There was a moment's pause, then a unanimous: "Yes, Mr. President." And the group departed.

It was not a difficult task to put down on paper what the President wanted. He had pictured the plight of trees and of young men in terms understandable and convincing. By nine o'clock the first draft of the bill which was to create the C.C.C. was ready, and the six men again sat with the President. The bill was read and discussed. Some changes were made. It was retyped and made ready to present to a group of Congressional leaders. They had been called for a ten o'clock meeting with the President. The idea of a Civilian Conservation Corps met with the approval of this group, who agreed to "steer" it through the two houses of Congress. When the six government officials left the President, the planning for the organization and operation of the C.C.C. already had begun. Thus was Emergency Conservation Work given first place in the new President's program of economic recovery.

A banking crisis had reared its head to occupy much of the attention of the President and Congress, but on March 21 a message from the President to Congress said, in part: "It is essential to our recovery program that measures immediately be enacted aimed at unemployment relief. A direct attack on this problem suggests three types of legislation . . .

"The first of these measures . . . can and should be immediately enacted. I propose to create a civilian conservation corps to be used in simple work, not interfering with normal employment, and confining itself to forestry, the prevention of soil erosion, flood control, and similar projects. I call your attention to the fact that this type of work is of definite practical value, not only through the prevention of great present financial loss but also as a means of creating future national wealth. This is brought home by the news we are receiving today of vast damage caused by floods on the Ohio and other rivers.

"Control and direction of such work can be carried on by existing machinery of the Departments of Labor, Agriculture, War, and Interior.

"I estimate that 250,000 men can be given temporary employment by early summer if you give me authority to proceed within the next two weeks. . . .

"This enterprise is an established part of our national policy. It will conserve our precious natural resources. It will pay dividends to the present and future generations. It will make improvements in National and State domains which have been largely forgotten in the past few years of industrial development.

"More important, however, than the material gains will be the moral and spiritual value of such work. The overwhelming majority of unemployed Americans, who are now walking the streets and receiving private or public relief, would infinitely prefer to work. We can take a vast army of these unemployed out into healthful surroundings. We can eliminate to some extent at least the threat that enforced idleness brings to spiritual and moral stability. It is not a panacea for all the unemployment, but it is an essential step in this emergency."

When the bill incorporating the ideas expressed in the President's message was turned over to the Committee on Education and Labor for consideration and report, the C.C.C. was given its first "acid test." There were many skeptics. The idea was new, and therefore untried. Would it amount to much more than a "dole" to young men who would be given "a vacation in the woods at government expense"? Would the wage of a dollar per day tend to lower the standard of wages in the country? It was organized labor that raised this question about wages. Others also thought the wage too small, suggesting various sums from $50 to $80 per month, and there were some who insisted that the work should not be restricted to unmarried men.

But those leaders who were acquainted with the President's ideas of the project insisted that it was not so much one of giving men employment at prevailing wages, as one of giving them a chance to direct their idle minds and hands to work. The relief for them and their families was of secondary importance. And the President won his point. Indeed, the bill was amended to give the President even wider powers than he had asked. The time of service and the rate of pay were left to his discretion. The amount of money made available for the work was the only restriction. Instead of work being limited to national forests and parks, its scope was widened to include also work on state, municipal, and private lands. On March 28 the Senate voted its approval of the amended bill for Emergency Conservation Work. The House did likewise, the following day. And thus was created the authority upon which the C.C.C. has been built.

Armed with this power, the President proceeded to create an organization of civilian workers which in size and speed of enrollment rivaled the mobilization of troops in time of war. The Department of Labor was given the task of selecting the young men who were to make up the C.C.C. The Departments of Agriculture and the Interior had to designate and direct the work to be done. The Department of War was charged with the responsibility of organizing the men into work groups, clothing them, feeding them, transporting them, and supervising their life in the camps. Each department was told that the President wanted the men at work at the earliest possible time. This meant the utmost co-ordination of these four government departments, something not common in government operation.

Such co-ordination required a directing head. He was appointed from the ranks of organized labor. On April 4, Robert Fechner, a vice president of the American Federation of Labor, agreed to become Director of Emergency Conservation Work. He understood the President's desire for speed in placing the men in their camps. On the same day he met with an advisory council, composed of members of the various co-operating government agencies. On April 5, orders went out from the Department of War to the commanding generals of the nine Army corps areas in the country to begin the enrollment of men. The following day, the first man was enrolled — in Pennsylvania. The first camp was established within a week. During the month, an average of 1530 were enrolled each day, and by the first of July 275,000 men were located in more than 1300 camps, spread throughout the land.

Two hundred and fifty thousand of these men were between the ages of 18 and 25. They had been selected from every state in the nation. They came from the large cities, from the towns, and from the countryside. They were chosen under the direction of the U. S. Department of Labor and turned over to the Army for enrollment. The Army examined them, gave them uniforms, conditioned them for life in the woods, took them into the forests, directed the building of their camps, and then turned them over to forestry superintendents for work.

Camps were of tents, located, for the most part, in national and state forests and parks. While the men were being selected and enrolled, the U. S. Forest Service and the National Park Service were designating the location of camp sites. There were millions of acres of forests in which needful work was available. The greater areas of forest land were in the West. The greater number of men were enrolled in the heavily populated states of the East and the Middle West. Several thousands of these first men were transported across the country to the mountains of Montana, Wyoming, Utah, Idaho, California, Washington, and Oregon.

Provision was made for the enrollment of a small number of men from the communities in which each camp was located. With the inclusion of about 25,000 war veterans and 14,000 Indians, this brought the strength of the C.C.C. to more than 300,000 men living in conservation work camps.

When time permitted, camps were built before the men were moved into them. But for many of the first camps men and tentage and equipment went on the same train or the same trucks. Many of the first camps, too, were put up in the night, and in mud and rain. Many meals were cooked in the open and eaten by men seated on fallen trees or the ground. It was not an easy life for the men from the cities, most of whom were now in the mountains and woods for the first time in their lives. They discovered that C.C.C. life was not just a "swell vacation at government expense." Many of them "couldn't take it," and "went over the hill." These were C.C.C. expressions. "Going over the hill" meant deserting.

It was all a new experience, getting a first taste of work and of discipline under Army officers, and living in a group of 200 men in a country where the stillness of nights, unbroken by the rumble of elevated trains or the bleat of foghorns, was almost terrifying. It was the first time away from home for most of the men, and homesickness played havoc with many of them. But hard work and regular sleep, with plenty of food and recreation, did much to clear their minds and nurture their morale. The first pay day helped; so did the first trip to town, in some places forty or fifty or one hundred miles away. Within a month the men had bared their backs to the sun and were bragging about the amount of work their particular crew or company did each day.

The summer of 1933 found more than 1400 camps established, with wooden barracks for mess hall and kitchen and for recreation purposes. The men got used to their work. They learned to destroy insects, clear dead timber snags, and build trails and mountain roads. Some were called upon to fight forest fires and construct erosion control dams. They became acquainted with discipline, the job of getting along with other men, and the meaning of manual labor. The President addressed a message of greeting to them: "I want to congratulate you on the opportunity you have, and extend to you my appreciation for the hearty co-operation you have given this greatest peacetime movement the country ever has seen." In August he announced that the men would be given a chance for re-enrolling for an additional six months' period. Nearly two thirds of them signed up for another "hitch" in the tree army that was then looking forward to a winter in the forests. The others went back home, some fortunate enough to have found a job, others to resume their quest for one, or to settle back into their old routine of "just waiting." Nearly 100,000 other men came in to fill the bunks and the places at the mess hall tables left vacant by these men; and the C.C.C. began its second lap of activity.

Men could not live in tents during the winter, except in a few of the Southern states. Wooden barracks had to be constructed for them. Some of the camps, those in the higher mountainous regions, had to be moved to a more temperate climate. Throughout the country groups of carpenters descended upon the camps and erected long barracks in which stoves were installed. The men were outfitted in long underwear, woolen clothes, and heavy shoes, and work went on, although the thermometer in many places dropped to several degrees below zero and many camps were snowed in for days at a time. When Thanksgiving came, there was turkey on every camp table. During the Christmas holidays the men were permitted to visit the homes which their wages were helping to support. They had changed, most of the men. Their life and work out of doors had put color in their faces, muscle on their bodies, and a new glint in their eyes.

The men had been given work to do, books to read, and equipment for athletic recreation. It was decided to give them also an opportunity to further their education. Some of the men had been forced to leave college and high school because of the condition of the family finances. Others had dropped out of school to go to work and had not been able to get a job. Some few had never gone to school, and could neither read nor write. An educational program that would serve all these men was planned by the Department of Education. More than 1,000 educational advisers were placed in the camps. They were young men, mostly, with an educational background. Their job was to help organize classes and discussion groups in the camps and in near-by towns. This afforded the men an opportunity of directed study during their leisure time. It also gave employment to the advisers who had been trained as teachers.

Another spring came. Camps were moved back into their mountain sites, and new ones were located. In April, the President extended the life of Emergency Conservation Work for another year. Another hundred thousand men were brought into the ranks of the C.C.C. to fill the places of those who left after the expiration of a year in the forests. By the summer of 1934 all the original C.C.C. enrollment, excepting a few of the locally enrolled men and the war veterans, had been sent back to their homes. A twelve-month maximum service period had been adopted, so as to give as many young men as possible an opportunity for work in the C.C.C. Then the drought hit the Middle West. Streams and pastures dried up and many farms were covered with sand carried by the wind. Thousands of young men who had found employment on these lands were now without hope of work. The President ordered enlargement of the C.C.C. by 50,000 to take care of these men. This increased its strength to more than 350,-000.

The work the men did increased in extent and quality. They had learned to swing an ax and use a brush hook. Forest fire loss was cut tremendously. Thousands of miles of fire break and trail and road and telephone lines now stretched across the forest lands from New England to Death Valley. The gypsy moth was being given the battle of its life along the Hudson River front, and thousands of men were at work checking the spread of blister rust and beetle through the valuable pine timber forests of the South and West. Bridges and dams and look-out towers built by the C.C.C. now numbered thousands. Erosion of fields in the Middle West was being held in check, mosquito-infested marsh lands were being drained, and streams were being made more inhabitable for fish and fowl. National and state parks were being made more accessible, and many great forests were being conserved and reclaimed.

Criticism of the work of the C.C.C. had subsided, and its worth was extolled in press and speech. Thousands of families were benefited financially by the wages the men earned, and the men were rehabilitated in body and spirit. When another Congress met in January of 1935, little argument was needed to convince its members of the value and possibilities of Emergency Conservation Work. The President, in his first message to this Congress, spoke of the success of the Civilian Conservation Corps and asked for its extension and its enlargement.

Emergency Conservation Work was begun as an experiment in conservation of forests and men. It became the most extensive peacetime project ever attempted by the federal government. Its worth was measured by its accomplishments. But its success has been due, in great part, to the co-ordination of the various independent government departments participating in its operation.

★ 2 ★

A FOUR-TEAM HITCH

THE economic life of the nation had dipped uncomfortably low by the spring of 1933. Those men who had jobs clung to them. They held tenaciously, even at reduced wages. It was almost impossible for a young man to break through the barricade which the depression had thrown up between him and what he considered his future. Especially true was this of those men who had had no experience at work. And there were many such between 18 and 25 years of age. Reaching a time in their lives when young men usually start in a trade or vocation or profession, these men found the trades and professions pared to skeleton forces and "No Help Wanted" signs tacked to factory and office doors. In fact, it had been so long since help had been wanted that many such signs had been made durable and permanent.

A large number of these young men in search of jobs were members of families already cutting down their expenses to keep off the relief rolls. The families of others were already on relief rolls, some of them for the first time in their lives. Boys from the country went to the towns looking for work. Boys of the towns went to the cities. Boys of the cities roamed from city to city. But they found "No Help Wanted" signs wherever they went. Many of them took to the highways, either for an adventurous something to do or to lighten the burden at home. Some were content to wander, but the great mass of them were willing and anxious to work. Little thought had been directed to their plight. Heads of families were given the first call for what little help was needed in industry or on the farms. It was for the younger generation of men that the Civilian Conservation Corps was formed. It was something new — a government creating jobs where there had been no jobs before. It was big news to these young men, that a quarter of a million of them would be given work. But it was a tremendous and far-reaching task for the government to shoulder.

There was much more to the organization of the C.C.C. than the driving of an Army truck through town, loading it with men, dumping them off at the nearest forest, and telling them to go to work. It was an undertaking comparable only to the mobilization of an army during the World War. And it was faced with many difficulties not experienced in 1917. Responsibility for selecting, training, and directing the new soldiers then rested solely with the War Department. The purpose was clear, and the rules and regulations well known. In 1933, however, four government departments were given the responsibility for the C.C.C. The purpose was more diffuse, and the rules and regulations were foreign to the handbook of any one department. The Army enrolled the men, yet the C.C.C. was strictly a civilian organization, and its members were selected under direction of the Department of Labor. The U. S. Forest Service and the National Park Service selected the work sites, but the Army supervised the building of the camps. The foresters supervised the work the men did; the Army paid them and directed their life in camp, but had nothing to say about their work. The purpose of the C.C.C. was to conserve natural resources, rehabilitate the bodies and minds of young men, and relieve the financial strain on their families at home.

Government departments rarely had been called upon to work in co-operation with one another. The function and purposes of each are rather definitely defined, even though two or more departments may in some respects do similar work. Each department has its own ambitions and manner of doing things. Subordination of these to the practices of another department seldom is done willingly, or with grace. To co-operate with other departments for the creation of an entirely new agency of government was a unique and significant experiment. No one of the four departments — Labor, War, Agriculture, the Interior — considered the C.C.C. its own "child." There was fear on the part of some that the child would grow up to be a wastrel, and possibly cast reflection on its parent. The C.C.C. needed an understanding godfather who would claim the infant as his own and assume the responsibility of its rearing. It needed a leader who could do what never had been done with any degree of success — coordinate the operations of four government departments. Such a man was chosen from the ranks of organized labor.

Robert Fechner, of Boston, general vice-president of the International Association of Machinists, was called to Washington by the President to assume the burden of directing Emergency Conservation Work. He, if anyone, should have understood the importance of a job to young men. He had gone to work when he was sixteen years of age and had been a member of the machinists' union for thirty-seven years. As a railroad machinist, he had traveled over a large part of the United States and Mexico and into Central and South America. Since 1914 he had been a member of the General Executive Board of the International Association of Machinists. He had played a prominent part in the 1901 fight for a nine-hour working day and in the 1915 eight-hour movement. He had lectured on labor economics at Harvard, Brown, and Dartmouth. He first met President Roosevelt in Washington during the World War.

There was another meeting between Mr. Fechner and the President on March 25, before Congress had acted on the bill giving the President authority to create the C.C.C. The President outlined his plan for a civilian conservation corps. He emphasized the humanitarian feature of the proposed work. It was that feature which decided Mr. Fechner to accept the task of unifying the operations of the various government departments which already were planning their parts in Emergency Conservation Work. An advisory council, consisting of representatives of the departments of Labor, War, Agriculture, and the Interior, had been designated by the President. With Director Fechner at its head, it was to function as a planning board, wrestling with the problems of men, supplies, transportation, work sites, equipment, and discipline.

On April 4, Director Fechner took over the reins of his four-team government "hitch" and "started for the forests." And it was at no easy canter. The President had said that he wanted the men in camp at the earliest day possible. He wanted the first camp established and occupied within a week. But before camps could be occupied, there had to be men to occupy them. There were several millions of young men in the country who were unemployed and worthy of a job. A comparatively small number could be given places in the first contingent of the C.C.C. The initial problem was to select 240,000 of the qualified and most deserving of these men. This was the part the Department of Labor was to play.

There was no time to set up a nation-wide organization to do this work, but there were unemployment-relief agencies in each state which needed only proper co-ordination to function adequately at a moment's notice. They were acquainted with a large number of the young men who needed jobs, and they were willing to act as representatives of the Department of Labor. The Department of Labor took up its task on April 3. By April 5, the state unemployment-relief agencies had been brought into the Emergency Conservation Work program. By April 6, they were ready to turn men over to the Army for enrollment. From then until July 1, when the last of the 240,000 men were enrolled, this group of agencies furnished qualified men as rapidly as the Army could induct them into the ranks of the C.C.C. The first 25,000 men were selected in the seventeen larger cities of the country, because of their immediate availability. The rest came from every city, town, and countryside of the entire nation.

Each state was assigned a quota of men, on the basis of population, with the largest number to New York and the fewest to Nevada. Each state agency then established quotas within its state on the same basis. Selection was to be made primarily from "physically fit unemployed unmarried men between the ages of 18 and 25 years, who are citizens of the United States, who have dependents, and who wish to allot to these dependents a substantial portion of the $30 monthly cash allowance." Young, unmarried men were to be selected partly because of the type of work and the camp life involved, and partly because they represented a group of workers who were finding it most difficult to secure employment. The work was to be for young men who had dependents and who wanted to help them, rather than for unattached, homeless, transient men. It was thought the money expended could be used more productively if it were to benefit whole families rather than single individuals. There was no definite rule as to the amount of his pay which each man was to allot to his family, but the men who expressed a desire to allot a large portion of it usually had the better chance of being selected. The average allotment was $25 per month. This was satisfactory to both the selecting agencies and those in charge of the camps, who thought the men in camp would not need more, but should not have less, than $5 per month for incidental expenses. In some instances a part of the money allotted to the family, and sent directly to it by the government, was returned to the man in camp. But this practice was frowned upon and made the man who received it subject to discharge.

The men were to be selected first, but not exclusively, from families then receiving aid from relief agencies. This was because the needs of those families were a matter of knowledge, and it would avoid wholesale registration, which would have necessitated an expensive and time-consuming investigation, and would have slowed up the process of selection. This did not, however, exclude a young man who would apply for a job and establish the fact that his family, although not then receiving relief, was actually in need of his wage to avoid public aid. Destitution in itself, however, was not a badge of acceptability. Selections were to be made on a basis of "fitness of the applicant and the greatest possible good to the community." Selection agencies were cautioned that the primary purpose was not to lighten their relief loads, but to make Emergency Conservation Work a success. Few of the agencies took advantage of this opportunity of shifting their other responsibilities to the federal government, and for the most part the men they selected for the C.C.C. were qualified, both from the standpoint of physical fitness and from that of family needs. Enrollment was to be wholly voluntary. No one was to be "drafted" or "conscripted" for the work. No one was to be urged to enroll in order to support his family. Only those applicants who were anxious to have a part in the project were wanted. Agencies could not force a man to apply for C.C.C. work on threat of having relief for his family stopped. There was little violation of these principles in the selection of the men. That many of the first group sent to camp were of the type who thought it would be a "vacation," and either deserted or were discharged for misconduct, was due principally to the speed at which they had to be selected in the early days of the C.C.C.

Because it was thought that each forest camp should be surrounded by a hospitable neighborhood, and that the moving in of a group of city boys to work, when many of the men of the community were without employment, would tend to create animosity, provision was made for the enrollment of a limited number of local men in each company. Age restrictions on these men were lifted, and both married and unmarried men were accepted. Many of them had had considerable experience in the forests and it was thought they would exercise wholesome leadership among the younger men. In all, about 35,000 of such men were taken into the ranks of the C.C.C. In addition, provision was made for the inclusion of war veterans, without age or marital restrictions. They represented about ten per cent of the entire enrollment. They were selected by the U. S. Veterans' Administration; but the first group of them were enrolled on President Roosevelt's invitation to veterans who had gone to Washington to plead the cause of a soldiers' bonus. Also there were enrolled some 14,000 Indians for Emergency Conservation Work on Indian reservations. They were selected and placed at work under the direction of the Bureau of Indian Affairs of the Department of the Interior. In addition, camps for 4,000 men were established in Puerto Rico, the Hawaiian Islands, Alaska, and the Virgin Islands.

During the first two years, more than 1,000,000 men were given employment in the C.C.C., exclusive of the Army officers, work superintendents and foremen, and specialized workers such as carpenters, plumbers, and electricians. The young men were enrolled for periods of six months, with the privilege of re-enrolling for another six months, but limited to a maximum of fifteen months of service. On enrollment, each man agreed to remain in the C.C.C. for six months, but provision was made to grant a man an honorable discharge if he had a chance to get permanent employment or if he furnished other sufficient reason. Regulations also called for dishonorable discharges for desertion or gross misconduct, such as refusal to work, violation of discipline, or misbehavior.

Before the men selected under direction of the Department of Labor could be placed at work in forest camps, they had to be enrolled by the Department of War. This was another task for the new director of Emergency Conservation Work and his advisory council. Few of the young men were physically prepared for manual labor. They had to be given a preliminary conditioning "workout" at Army posts to fit them for work. They had to be outfitted with clothes and equipment. They had to be transported to work camps. But before there could be work camps, there had to be work sites selected for the camps. This was a job for the Department of Agriculture and the Department of the Interior, and involved another problem of co-ordination.

There were millions of acres of forest and park lands in the country. There was hardly an acre of it that did not need some attention such as a group of young foresters could give it. There was plenty of work to be done, fighting disease and pests that destroy forests, checking fires that burned in an hour or a day trees that it took years to grow, reforesting lands already cleared of timber by fire and man. There was no scarcity of work; the difficulty was one of "where to work?" Some of the forests were under the supervision of the Forest Service, of the Department of Agriculture; some were under the National Park Service, of the Department of the Interior. Much of the forest land, however, was under state and private ownership. Co-operation between state and federal governments is not always a simple matter. There were differences to adjust. One of them was the physical location of each camp site. Many things were involved. It was desirable that the men should accomplish the greatest amount of work possible during their stay in the woods; it was not feasible to place camps too far from work locations. The camps had to be accessible; men and equipment had to be hauled to the camp. The men had to be fed; camps could not be cut off from sources of food and water. Some of the early camps, however, had to be established a hundred miles or more from the nearest town.

It was comparatively easy for officials of the Forest Service and the National Park Service to designate locations on their own lands. But it was more difficult to deal with state parks and forests. And in the East, where the greater number of men were being enrolled, the forests and parks were mostly owned by the states. The governor of each state was informed of the plans for conservation work to be done by the Civilian Conservation Corps, and invited to participate in the project. All that was necessary, in the form of compensation, was that the state agree to share with the federal government a portion of the increased value which would accrue to the state through the work of the C.C.C. Some states saw the opportunities in such work more readily than others did. Some of them grasped at the chance of "playing host" to outfits of the new Civilian Conservation Corps. But even in these states, each work project and each camp site had to be inspected and approved. The work which the C.C.C. was authorized to do was limited. It could build forest trails and roads to permit access of fire fighters, but it was not allowed to enter into highway construction. It could clear lands of fire hazards and disease-carrying underbrush, but was not to clear private lands to permit a farmer to cultivate more of his farm — as was urged by one request sent in to Washington. It could fight the gypsy moth and the pine beetle, but it was not to enter into competition with professional tree surgeons. Each work project was recommended by either the Department of Agriculture or the Department of the Interior and then approved by Director Fechner and his advisers.

President Roosevelt had told Director Fechner that he wanted the first camp established and manned within a week. It was at Luray, Virginia, in the George Washington National Forest. It was established under conditions which prevailed for many weeks during the first months of the C.C.C. — days of rain and mud. This first outfit, composed of boys from the city, made the trek into the mountains in trucks, at night and in the rain. They had to light their way with lanterns to keep themselves from slipping from the mud-covered roads. They had to detour in places because of unsafe bridges across the Shenandoah. Arrived at the site of their camp, they had to set up tents in the dark. It continued to rain the following day, and there was more mud. It took a lot of "can take it" to carry these men through that day, and there was much talk that night of "going over the hill." But the next day the sun came out, and the morale of the men mounted with the temperature. The first camp of this new conservation army had been saved by the sun, as it had been threatened by the rain.

Other camps were established rapidly, many of them under similar conditions, and more men were moved into the Army conditioning camps. Enrollment of men and the movement of men from home to Army post, from conditioning camp to work camp, from the cities of the East to the mountains of the West, continued unbroken until the last man was en- rolled and started for his job in the forests, on July 1. The undertaking resembled, in many ways, the enlistment of an army in time of war. It was an army, headed for a great peacetime war against depression and against the exploita- tion and destruction of a nation's forests. But no army moves without equipment. The C.C.C. needed clothes, food, tents, stoves, trucks, tractors, ambulances, axes and saws. It needed discipline — concerted action for a common good. It needed at its back a community friendly to the "strangers" moving in. The ultimate success of the C.C.C. depended upon the com- pleteness and efficiency of this phase of the work. And this was the job of the Department of War.

THE ROOKIE   26

⋆ 3 ⋆

PEACETIME WAR

THE U. S. Army has done much pioneer work in the development of the nation. Roads and bridges over which early settlers went to the West were built by the Army, and the Army protected the travelers while they were on their way and after they had established their settlements. The important Lewis and Clark expedition into the far Northwest was an Army undertaking. When it came time to link the Western outposts of civilization with the East, the Army located and made possible the operation of the first railroads. Army engineers planned the early canals of the country which for years were important routes of commerce, and developed the great waterways of the nation. The Army made possible, through protection by arms, the building up of the Pacific Coast, and, through its engineers and troops, the development of the gold fields of Alaska. The Ordnance Department, Signal Corps, Air Service, and Chemical Warfare Service of the Army have blazed the trail for many of the large private industries of today — such as steel, the telegraph and telephone, aviation, and dye and commercial gas industries. The Medical Corps of the Army made it possible for Army engineers to build the Panama Canal, by making Panama a safe place in which to work, and it gave the world its first definite information that led to the control of yellow fever. But the most extensive peacetime operation of the U. S. Army has been its role in Emergency Conservation Work.

For eight hours each day, five days a week, the 350,000 men of the C.C.C. are "on the job" and under the direction of work superintendents. Every other hour of the day, and night, these men are supervised, cared for, and guided by the U. S. Army. The Army is their provider and tailor, doctor and teacher, spiritual adviser and paymaster. It took the men selected by the Department of Labor, examined them, conditioned them, clothed them, moved them into camps which it supervised and equipped, provided the men with three meals a day, gave them recreational and educational advantages, doctored them, disciplined them, and paid them at the end of each month. The federal government was Uncle Sam to the men, but the Army became their "Uncle Bud."

The Department of War got an early start in its preparation for Emergency Conservation Work. When, on April 3, 1933, the President asked the Army whether it could begin the enrollment of men within three days, it replied, without hesitation, that it could. The Army could have made that promise a week before Congress passed the necessary authorization for the C.C.C. In fact, it had its basic plans ready before the President announced his conservation program. A month earlier, in Congress, a bill had been introduced which provided that the Army should take over the task of sheltering and feeding several thousands of unemployed and transient youths of the country. When the Army saw that it might be called upon to perform this emergency function, it began to make preparations. Its plans were made, but the bill was not enacted into law by Congress. When the President told the Army of his desire to create a civilian conservation corps, out came these plans from the Army's archives. They formed the basis of its operations with the C.C.C.

The U. S. Army that entered Emergency Conservation Work was not the same Army that entered the World War. The National Defense Act of 1920 had given the United States, for the first time, a definite military policy. It was the result of lessons learned in the World War. By the time the war on depression began, the Army was functioning on an entirely different theory of organization. The country had been divided into nine Army Corps Areas. Each, under the command of a major general, had become, for Army purposes, a kingdom in itself. The corps area commanding officer was supreme, except in matters of general policy. He was responsible only to "G.H.Q." in the Department of War in Washington. Here the general policies and objectives of the Army were formulated. Their execution was decentralized to the nine corps. The corps area commander played the War Department's role in his province. But there had been no opportunity for a real test of the effectiveness of this Army set-up. The enrollment and command of 300,000 men of the C.C.C. — greater in size and scope than that which attended mobilization during the Spanish-American War — afforded the Department of War a chance to try it out.

When a boy was selected for enrollment in the ranks of the C.C.C., he was told to take a lunch along and report to Army recruiting officials at a definite place and time. The Army assumed responsibility for him there. It gave him a preliminary physical examination and transported him to one of half a hundred conditioning camps, spread throughout the country, vaccinated and inoculated him against contagious diseases, recorded him, outfitted him with clothes, fed him, housed him, and prepared him for the rigors of camp life. Then the Army transported him, by either truck, bus, or train to one of the work camps, some of which were located 3,000 miles away and many miles from post office or railroad station. The Army had prepared plans for the building of the work camp, had furnished the tents or lumber from which it was built, and supervised its building. Here, it provided the man with bed and bedding, procured and prepared his food, organized his recreation and furnished him with athletic equipment, directed his education, provided him medical and hospital service, paid him his allowance at the end of each month, sent his allotment to his family, and, after his term of enrollment was completed, transported him back home. This took personnel, ability, and organization.

During the first three months of the World War, the Army mobilized 181,000 men. During a like period in 1933, it enrolled 275,000 men, organized them into 1,315 companies of 200 men each, and established them in forest camps throughout the country. Each company was originally provided with two Regular Army officers, one Reserve Corps officer, and four Regular Army enlisted men, mostly non-commissioned officers. There were approximately but 12,000 officers in the Regular Army. They were scattered throughout the United States and our insular possessions, in command of troops, instructing National Guard, Organized Reserve and Reserve Officer training groups, at Army schools, and attached to General Staff and service duties in Washington and at corps area headquarters. More than 3,000 of these officers were called from their instructional details and placed on C.C.C. duty. In addition, 1,800 Reserve Corps officers were placed on active duty with the C.C.C. units, and 500 Regular Navy and Marine Corps officers were "drafted" to help organize C.C.C. outfits. Likewise, there was hardly a branch or arm of the Army that was not called upon to curtail its regular functions and assist in the organization or service of Emergency Conservation Work. These Regular Army officers with the companies gradually were replaced by Reserve Corps officers, as the camps became established and the routine of organization was made more permanent. Regular Army officers, however, were kept in corps area and district commands.

The use of Reserve Corps officers was doubly beneficial. It tended to relieve unemployment and also gave the Reserve officers an opportunity of training in practical leadership and command of men and in camp organization and control. For, as authority was decentralized from the General Staff to Corps Area commanders, so was it further delegated to district and sub-district commands, and to individual company commanders. And these company commanders, practically all of whom later were Reserve Corps officers, were to become the backbone of the entire C.C.C. organization. The success of Emergency Conservation Work — especially that phase directed to rehabilitating human resources — is largely dependent upon the commanding officers of the companies. Each commanding officer is father to the men under him, as well as being leader, adviser, and disciplinarian. He is responsible for every phase of the life of the men in camp, except for the time they are at work under supervision of forestry foremen. He is responsible for the physical camp, the purchasing and preparing of food for the men, and for their clothing and personal equipment. He designates the time when they shall go to bed and when they shall get up. He buys their magazines and newspapers and directs their recreational and educational programs. He must maintain harmonious relations between the camp and the surrounding community. He must preserve discipline of his men, both while in camp and while on "leave" to near-by towns and cities, yet his authority for discipline is not that which governs troops of the Army.

But if a company commander is ordered to take his outfit from, say, Camp Dix, New Jersey, to Missoula, Montana, he does not personally hail a train, load his men on, and then buy sandwiches and coffee for them along the route. The train will be awaiting him and his men at a designated place at a definite time. It will be provided with facilities for feeding and caring for the company until it reaches its destination. The Army has experts in transportation — an important factor in the organization of any military undertaking. And transportation was a tremendously important factor in the organization of the C.C.C. Men had to be transported from the conditioning camps to their work camps. About 54,000 men and officers were sent from Eastern and Middle Western states to the Far West during the early months of the C.C.C. These men were moved in 165 special trains. They were entrained at 25 different conditioning camps and dispatched to 159 different points of destination. And later, they had to be brought back again. Railroads, trucks, and busses were utilized in getting the men to their jobs. Few camps were located near the railroads. The majority of them were so situated that trucks had to supplement rail service. Some of the camps were in state parks adjacent to towns and cities, but the greater number were hidden away in the mountains. Many of them were from 50 to 100 miles from railroads and towns, and not a few at the end of insecure, treacherous forest roads.

Nor was the job of transportation ended when the men were set down in their first camps. At the close of each six months' period many camps had to be moved into new locations, either to new work projects, or because of too severe weather. Some of the outfits which were sent from New York, New Jersey, Ohio, Indiana, Kentucky, and Illinois to Utah, Wyoming, Montana, and Idaho, were moved to camp sites in Tennessee and Florida when snow and zero weather hit the western mountains.

Not only were there men to transport, but also camp equipment and supplies. For young men working in the mountains and getting plenty of sleep at night eat heartily and wear out clothes. Responsibility for clothing, housing, and feeding the men was vested in the Army. Preceding the entrance of the United States into the World War, there were months when such an eventuality seemed probable. This gave the Army an opportunity of preparing for the job of clothing "troops" on short notice. But the Army's participation in such an undertaking as Emergency Conservation Work began without much warning. Almost over night, comparatively, the Army was called upon to outfit a conservation corps of 250,-000 men. There was a limited supply of clothing in Army reserve depots, kept for use in an emergency. These regulation Army uniforms were utilized, through feats of emergency tailoring aimed at erasing their military character. The men of the C.C.C. were not of uniform physical size. Many of them were undersized. Consequently, the early arrivals in the ranks of this new forest army would not have had a chance of "getting by" a Regular Army inspection. But what they lacked in individual length or breadth, they made up in numbers. The C.C.C. outnumbered the Regular Army, three to one. Army depot factories worked day and night shifts to supply clothes and shoes. But they could not supply them in quantities needed in so short a time. Orders were placed with scores of private manufacturers for millions of articles of clothing — pants, underwear, shoes, shirts, raincoats, boots, besides toothbrushes, soap and other accouterment. One garb came into common use. It sprang from the Army "fatigue" uniform — pants and jumper of denim, and a hat of the same material, with wide, flapping brim. These were issued for use by the men while at work. Thousands of yards of denim had to be manufactured and made into these suits for the C.C.C. When winter came on, there were heavy underwear and socks to be furnished, and woolen overcoats, leather and wool windbreakers, heavy gloves, and overshoes. There was more time for the purchase and manufacture of these, and they added considerably to the appearance of the C.C.C. Many of the men had spent from their $5 a month to have their clothes tailored to fit them better. Many styles of pants and blouses came from these individual alterations by town and city tailors according to the fashion ideas of the men themselves.

But clothing was only a part of the equipment which the Army had to furnish for operation of C.C.C. camps. The early camps were of tents, taken from Army warehouses and transported to the forest camp sites. Later a wooden building was constructed to serve as mess hall and kitchen, and another to be used for recreation. When cold weather came, and the men could not be housed in tents, except in warm climates, wooden barracks had to be constructed. Plans for these were prepared by the Army, lumber was purchased by the Army, and the Army supervised the civilian workmen who constructed them. Kitchens had to have stoves, pans, griddles, and other utensils needed for cooking. Mess kits were used by the men at first, but these gradually were replaced with dishes. The tents and barracks had to be outfitted with beds, sheets, pillow cases, and blankets. The camps could not be operated without light and heat. Heating stoves were installed in the barracks, and if commercial power was not available, generating plants were provided for electric power. Trucks were needed to transport equipment and men. These had to be purchased and kept in running condition. There had to be ambulances, one for each four or five camps, to carry patients to hospitals in cases of serious illness or accident. These were matters which tested the supply organization of the Army. Finally there had to be a proper supply of food. The Army learned soon after the C.C.C. came into the forest that these men were better eaters than men of the Regular Army. Army rations were not sufficient for men who had worked all day building roads or clearing fire breaks.

The Army had to build up and sustain a maintenance system which reached into every state in the Union, up mountain roads and across marshes. Staple foods could be purchased and stored at convenient points for distribution, but keeping the many widely-separated camps in fresh meats and vegetables was another matter. Organization of a high order is essential to the successful management of so extensive a service. It has been accomplished through the decentralized Army system. Corps Area commanders were held responsible for the proper and adequate feeding of the men in their respective corps areas, district commanders for their districts, and company commanders for their companies. What did the General Staff in Washington say about the feeding of the men? It said that the food should be of definite grade and quantity, that it should be adequately prepared and should cost "so much." These standards were authorized by the director of Emergency Conservation Work. It was up to each Corps Area commander to see that such instructions were executed. The allowance for food was between 32 and 40 cents per day per man, depending on local conditions and prices — with turkey for Thanksgiving and Christmas dinners.

All this food and the clothing and equipment had to be paid for. How was this done? By the Army. The Army pays all the bills for the entire program, from funds allotted to Emergency Conservation Work and made available to the War Department by the U. S. Treasury. Equipment and supplies needed in large quantities are purchased in Washington or at the several Army depots. All other buying is delegated to Corps Area commanders, but some of the purchasing is passed on to district, sub-district, and company commanders, depending upon the organization and conditions prevailing in each corps area. The Ninth Corps area, for instance, which embraces the states of California, Washington, Oregon, Idaho, Montana, Nevada, and Utah, cannot be guided by conditions prevailing in less widely-scattered corps areas, such as the First, made up of the New England states. The Army also disburses funds to the Departments of Labor, Agriculture, and the Interior for their own Emergency Conservation Work personnel and their purchases of technical equipment. It pays the Reserve officers on C.C.C. duty from Emergency Conservation Work funds; it pays the men, sends their allotment checks home, and banks money for the war veterans in the camps.

But "man cannot live by bread alone." Important as food, clothing, and shelter are in C.C.C. camps, the men have time, need, and desire for other things — for recreation, for education, and for religious services. The Army must provide opportunity for all of these. Thousands of the men are located many miles from the nearest town or city. The men are accustomed to "movies," to athletics, and to other forms of social life. Athletic equipment is provided in each camp, and organized athletic programs are maintained. Men are transported into town at frequent intervals, and libraries have been established in each camp. There is a permanent library of general topics, and circulating or "traveling" libraries of fiction. Funds also are provided for the purchase of current magazines and newspapers. An extensive educational program has been set up in the camps, under the direction of the Army, but with the co-operation of the U. S. Department of Education, an agency of the Department of the Interior. The Army also is charged with affording the men an opportunity for religious expression. Some 200 Army chaplains are on duty with the C.C.C. Their job is of the circuit-riding variety, each chaplain having about eight camps under his advisory care. Protestant, Roman Catholic, and Jewish faiths are represented in their ranks. In addition, ministers and priests and rabbis of surrounding communities supplement the work done by the chaplains. The chaplains conduct services and direct religious programs for the men who are interested in religion. Some chaplains also act as welfare officers and are guiding figures in the organization of camp activities and camp spirit.

One of the most important and highly successful functions of the Army, however, is that of its medical service. More than "open spaces" and trees are needed to make the forests healthful places in which to reside, especially when one has to live in close contact with 200 or more other persons. Life in the woods and mountains can be healthful only when camp conditions are sanitary and men adhere to rules of personal good health. Contaminated water can disable a whole company of men in a week. So can food not stored and prepared under proper sanitary regulations. One man can infect a whole camp with disease if not properly cared for or removed from camp for hospitalization. The Army began administering to the men when they were presented for enrollment. Each man was examined for disease and physical disabilities. The Army learned during the World War that approximately half of the young men of the country suffer some physical defect. At conditioning camps the men were vaccinated against smallpox and inoculated against typhoid and paratyphoid. Medical men of the Army followed them into the camps. There, they had the two-fold responsibility — keeping the camp a healthful place in which to live, and keeping the men well or caring for them if they became sick or were injured. The Army is, in this respect, a "life extension institute." The C.C.C. men not only are protected and cared for against disease and injury, but they are taught the principles of personal hygiene, sanitation, and first aid.

Instruction in first aid is afforded every man in camp. He is taught the fundamentals of emergency treatment for wounds, snakebite, sunstroke, near-drowning, and the like. He is taught the use of the tourniquet, and how to apply it to stop blood flow. Many lives have been saved by enrollees through timely administration to others who have cut themselves with axes or saws, have had their legs or arms broken by falls or falling trees, have gone swimming and nearly drowned, or have been bitten by poisonous snakes.

Accident prevention, too, forms a large part of each camp's instruction program. Systematic effort, directed from the office of the Emergency Conservation Work in Washington, constantly is being made to keep the work in the woods as safe as possible. But there are accidents, and when men are hurt they are afforded immediate medical or surgical attention. Hospitalization, either in camp or in government or private hospitals, is provided for those men who require it. Ambulances are kept in readiness for emergencies, and even the airplane has been used to transport C.C.C. men to hospitals. The rate of sickness and fatality from sickness in the Civilian Conservation Corps has been kept below that which persisted in camps during the World War.

The Army knew, and the Director of Emergency Conservation Work knew, that conservation work could be done only by healthy men. And there was much work to be done in the forests and parks of the country, on erosion-swept hillsides, and along the streams and in the marshes. A new army had sprung up — a peacetime army. It was recruited to reclaim and rehabilitate the country's natural resources, which had been despoiled by man, fire, and rain.

ON THE TRAIL

★ 4 ★

TIMBER AND BEAUTY

ABOUT one third the area of the United States is in forests, or is potential forest land. Nearly three fourths of this land is under private ownership. The remainder, approximately 200,000,000 acres, is in possession of the federal and state governments. This is a vast possible reservoir of health, wealth, and pleasure, almost inexhaustible in depth, which can be tapped for all the citizens of the Nation, and the many more to be born. Most of the land is in national forests — 170,000,000 acres — located mainly in the mountainous regions of the country. There are 145 such forests. They are chiefly in the western states, from the Rocky Mountains to the Pacific coast. Colorado, northern Idaho, and western Montana abound in them. A comparatively few are scattered through the uplands of the East and in the northern Middle West. As national reserves, they are young. For only about forty years has the nation taken an interest in the forests of its own estates. As a source of national wealth and well-being, their future worth is inestimable.

Older, under government control, than national forests, are our national parks. The first one dates back to 1872. In comparison with the forests, however, their extent is small. They cover but 15,000,000 acres. But their development as scenic and recreational preserves has led the world. They, too, are located generally in the mountains, but, including other national reservations of allied nature, they are more evenly distributed between the eastern and western states. In the East, they are distributed from Maine to the tip of Florida. In the West are located the larger and more im-

39

portant ones. Together they form a public park system unparalleled in the annals of civilization.

The remainder of these 200,000,000 acres of forest land represent our state forests of 10,000,000 acres, and state parks of about 4,500,000 acres. Nearly half of this state park area is in one state. But the state park system of the United States is just beginning to grow.

Fire and reckless cutting were destroying a wide swath through the spruce, juniper, pine, and fir of the public domain as late as forty years ago, without the federal government making any systematic effort to protect them. They were left to burn, or to pass into the hands of exploiters. The first forest "reserve" was created by Congress in 1891. Later a system of management and organization was set up, and the forests were placed under the direction, first of the Department of the Interior, then of the Department of Agriculture. Scientific forestry then began to provide for new crops of timber when one was cut, restricted unbridled grazing that was ruining the range, and planned for the maintenance of water supply. It was not until 1907, however, that they became "national forests." It then had become evident that under government management there could be effected a sound economic and industrial development of the large timber areas of the public domain, which had not been attained on lands under private ownership.

But by the time this was recognized, nearly all of our national timber land in the eastern part of our country had passed into private ownership or, in small portion, to the states. The poor lands left were considered inadequate for the public need. The purchase of land for the protection of the headwaters of the navigable streams was necessary. Other purchases were made for the furthering of timber production. As these lands came into the hands of the federal government, they were put under systematic management. The timber alone on the eastern national forests now has greater value than the cost of acquiring the lands, although much of this land had been depleted by lumbering and fire while it was held in private ownership.

The latest impetus to be given the development of the national forest system was in 1934 and 1935 when President Roosevelt allotted $30,000,000 of emergency funds for the purchase of small tracts of timber land to "round out" existing national forests.

National forests differ from national parks chiefly in the purpose for which they were created. National parks are maintained for the preservation of outstanding scenic and recreational values. National forests were reserved for the maintenance of a variety of social and economic values in the public interest. In the forests, timber is a crop; to be grown and harvested in much the same manner as a field of wheat. There is a yearly lumber cut in our national forests of more than a billion feet. But lumbering is not the only, nor perhaps the most important, intent of national forestry. The protection of watersheds and the furnishing of pasture, likewise, are significant aims of systematic forestry. Our national forests protect about one third of the water-power resources of the country, ensure an adequate supply of pure water to hundreds of cities and towns, and furnish pasture for nearly 14,000,000 head of livestock. Recreational use of the forests is co-ordinated with its economic use.

But national forests are for the use of the people — for the permanent good of the whole people rather than for the temporary benefit of individuals or companies, as was the practice half a century ago. Agriculture and the industries of lumbering, mining, and the raising of livestock depend directly upon a permanent supply of water, wood, and forage. Making these accessible is the business of those directing national forests.

The amount of water and the manner in which it flows from the mountains affect the future development of the nation. Undoubtedly the greatest value of the mountain ranges of the country, many large areas of which are within national forests, lies in their influence upon the regularity of the water supply. Vegetal covering, such as forests, has a decided influence on the "run-off" of water. Floods are the disastrous consequences of too rapid a "run-off" from denuded uplands. The Tennessee River valley is an example of what exploitation of timber lands does to the future life of a region, affecting it for many miles away. Forests also hold the soil. The lack of vegetation, particularly on steep slopes, affords the soil no other adherence than that of friction, and it easily is carried downhill by the rains. Once this soil is lost, nothing remains to keep the water in check.

There are, of course, many recreational advantages found in our national forests. Millions of persons visit them every year, for camping, hunting, and fishing. Forests add materially to the development of wild life. There are several natural game refuges in the national forests and others are being created.

Opportunity for recreation, however, together with the preservation of natural scenery for esthetic reasons, is the idea behind the development of our national parks. In 1872, this idea was little more than an ideal. It first was expressed around a camp fire in the Yellowstone country, by a group of men who had gone into the region to verify rumors of gigantic hot springs and geysers, brought out by Indians and a few white trappers. Preservation of the beauty spots of the country against utilitarian development was a new conception of land use. This Yellowstone section was the first to come under control of the federal government and maintained as a national park. The hot springs of Arkansas, however, had been in possession of the government since 1832, but that was for their medicinal value. This idea of public management of lands for esthetic values now has spread throughout the world.

The National Park Service, a bureau of the Department of the Interior, was established in 1916, to manage these national parks, and allied federal reservations. In 1933 nearly all the land areas of such nature were placed under the control of this bureau, to be administered in a unified system. In all, there are twenty-four national parks, sixty-eight national monuments, eleven national military parks, eleven national cemeteries, ten battlefield sites, one national historical park, and four miscellaneous memorials.

Preservation of unusual scenery or natural wonder, or some historical or scientific feature of natural interest, is the purpose behind the national park development. Each national park represents the highest type of its particular feature found in the country, and duplication of such features is avoided in enlarging the system. Commercialism does not enter into park creation. Many of the parks contain great forests, but the value of the trees is in their beauty and not in their potentialities as lumber. Often the most beautiful ones are of little commercial value. There are many great waterfalls in the parks, but they are to feed man's hunger for beauty, rather than for power. There are wild animals in abundance, but they are not considered as possible food supply. All hunting, except "with a camera," is forbidden. To keep the natural beauty of the mountains, the forests, and the lakes unspoiled and within easy access of the public is the important function of proper park management.

Although the national monuments are more numerous and more widely scattered than the parks, their significance is not so much that of either beauty or recreation, as of historic or scientific meaning. They are of great variety — from the ruined dwellings of men who lived a thousand or more years ago, to areas made historic during the past century; from plants and trees now petrified, to magnificent groves of living trees. The range of national park and monument landscaping is as diversified as are "dog kennels in Alaska and colonial plantations in Virginia or as adobe houses with the cactus gardens in the southwest, and subarctic roadside planting in Maine." Nor is the national park system completed. Eventually, it is thought, this national gallery of scenic, historic, and scientific displays will be much enlarged. Additional areas now are under consideration.

National parks have become the recreational centers for millions of people each year. They tour through them, camp within their majestic beauty, or stay in the hotels which have been erected in some of the larger parks. They find recreation for body and mind from living in the romantic and magnificent splendor of nature and meeting face-to-face the many wild animals the like of which their pioneer forefathers encountered when moving in to open the West. Animals that once roamed a large portion of the whole country now are found only in zoological cages or in the national parks. These parks are sanctuaries for many animals. Hunting is not permitted in any of them. Buffalo, bear, elk, antelope, deer, moose, and mountain sheep add much to the natural attraction of these government reserves. Bird conservation also is an important function of national park management. Some of the almost extinct varieties are being protected and developed in the "cover" which the parks afford. Although hunting is prohibited, fishing is permitted under regulations which insure against depletion of the fish supply. Many of the waters which were barren when the parks were organized now have become good fishing spots, through systematic propagation and restocking. Even the semidesert Grand Canyon streams are becoming an angler's paradise.

Most of the national parks, and a large number of the monuments, are located in the mountains, where forest, stream, valley, and craggy precipices combine with the glaciers and the sun to make them fairylands of reality. Yellowstone National Park, mostly in Wyoming, but partly in Idaho and Montana, is perhaps the best-known and the most visited of the parks. With its great geysers, numbering more than in all the rest of the world together, its colorful hot springs, its scenic canyon, its foaming Yellowstone River pouring from pine-clad hills and breaking over jagged rocks, this encampment of nature's phenomena is one of the great splendor displays of the world. And only eleven miles south, in the great Teton Mountains, is Grand Teton National Park. Rising above historic and romantic Jackson Hole, and in greater contrast because of the absence of foothills, eleven peaks lift grey precipices like cathedrals into the perennial snows of their tops.

Three large national parks grace the Sierra uplands of central California — Yosemite, Sequoia, and General Grant. Yosemite, with its granite wilderness, its spectacular waterfalls, beside which Niagara is a midget, its singing streams and innumerable lakes and snowy mountains, is the largest of the three. Its moderate summer weather, with cool, starry nights, and the supreme beauty of its valley, attract hundreds of thousands of visitors each season. Sequoia and General Grant are the parks of the Big Trees. The magnificent conifer forests and many groves of sequoias which abound here, and Mt. Whitney, the highest in the United States, are but part of the attraction of these west coast parks.

To the extreme north are Rainier and Glacier national parks, the former in Washington, the latter extending along the Canadian border in Montana. Glaciers, dense forests, mountains, and flowers give Rainier its beauty. Mt. Rainier, 14,408 feet high, gives it stateliness. Its glaciers, larger and more impressive than any others in the United States, add to its splendor. There are 48 square miles of glaciers here — some of them pushing over precipices like waterfalls. And also, there are wild flower parks at the base of Mt. Rainier that stretch far up its icy finger valleys. Paradise Valley is one of them, and well named. Farther east, beyond the tip of Idaho that separates the states, is Glacier National Park in Montana. Here, in romantic setting, are sixty smaller glaciers and hundreds of lakes surrounded by a richly colored land of gigantic cirques. There is no scenic spot in the country to compare with this great park.

To the south, in southern Oregon and in northern California, are the two great volcanic national parks. The Lassen Volcanic Park in California surrounds Mt. Lassen, and here is the only place in the country where the phenomena of recent volcanic activity can be observed. Primeval forests cover nearly the entire area, and impressive canyons, Alpine lakes, and many falls contribute to its beauty. Crater Lake National Park, in Oregon, is a show place. Crater Lake, 2,000 feet deep in places, has 250 square miles of rugged picturesqueness. It lies in the crater of an extinct volcano, has no known outlet, and is surrounded by fine forests of hemlock and fir and yellow pine.

Desert and semidesert national parks are those of Utah and Arizona. Grand Canyon, the unparalleled spectacle, the "18-

by 217-mile paint pot," stretches for 56 miles through Grand Canyon National Park in Arizona, with the Colorado River eating deeper into its precipitous gorge each year. Across the Utah border are Zion National Park and Bryce Canyon National Park, the former with its fantastically carved sandstone cliffs whose vermilion precipices "brighten more than 100 desert miles." In Bryce Canyon are the famous Pink Cliffs, their rock among the most colorful on earth.

But it is granite, not sandstone, that forms the "Rockies" and the Continental Divide in Colorado, where Rocky Mountain National Park is situated. Longs Peak, more than 14,000 feet high, rises above its 11,000-foot brothers to command the pine-, aspen-, and Columbine-strewn "low land," itself more than a mile above sea level. One may witness a thunderstorm born and dissipated on the top of Longs Peak within five minutes, can marvel at the sunset and the sunrise reflected on the face of these lofty granite upheavals, or may catch glimpses of bighorn sheep, more agile than the celebrated chamois of the Swiss Alps.

In the southwestern corner of Colorado is Mesa Verde National Park, where the story of the cliff-dwelling civilization and the history of the Indians before them are written in an anthropologist's paradise. Evidence of the Mongoloid hunters of over ten thousand years ago has been discovered here. And, too, here are the remains of the cliff-dwellers' culture — a story of the hard living of those early times. Here also are the mesas, with Mesa Verde the largest — fifteen miles long, eight miles wide, and from three hundred to five hundred feet high.

There are two governmental spring water reservations among the national parks. One, the Platt National Park, in Oklahoma, and in a part of what once was the Choctaw nation, is known for its numerous hot and cold springs of sulphur, iron, and bromide water. The other, and one of the best-known of all the bathing resorts, is the Hot Springs National Park of Arkansas. Hot water of accredited medicinal value pours from forty-six springs which abound in the Hot Spring mountain region of almost 1,000 acres.

Caves, too, have become part of the national park system. Wind Cave National Park, in the southwest corner of South Dakota, is surrounded by fossil deposits of prehistoric alligators, rhinoceroses, and three-toed horses; and by lofty, needlelike formations that erosion has sculptured in the masses of granite high up the forest-clad slopes of the Black Hills. The wind cave is in the limestone formations. The wind which races in and out of the entrance, depending upon the changing atmospheric pressure outside, gives the cave its name. The Carlsbad Caverns National Park, in New Mexico, is thought to be the largest series of connected caverns in the world. Its interior is one of majestic limestone decorations, and it is located in a semidesert country of unusual cactus vegetation. In it, Bat Cave is the daytime rendezvous for millions of bats that emerge every night, forage for insects, and return before the following daybreak.

In the eastern states there are but few national parks. Acadia National Park comprises a group of granite mountains rising from an island near the coast of Maine. Near-by headlands also are included in this reserve, which has been donated to the federal government by private owners. This is the only prominent elevation along the entire Atlantic coast. Its scenic beauty is that afforded by a mingling of mountains and the sea. In Tennessee and North Carolina is the national park of the Great Smoky Mountains. This includes the most massive mountain uplift in eastern United States and is a popular recreation spot for both the hunter and the hiker. It once was the great hunting grounds of the Cherokee Indians.

Among the newest national parks are the Abraham Lincoln National Park in Kentucky and the Ft. McHenry National Park, in Maryland, recently transferred to the National Park Service from control by the War Department. The former includes the one-room log cabin in which Lincoln was born, and part of the old Lincoln farm. Ft. McHenry is noted because the defeat of the British fleet here was largely responsible for the successful termination of the War of 1812. Here it was, too, that Francis Scott Key composed "The Star-Spangled Banner."

The Morristown national historical park, New Jersey, was acquired in 1933, and is important because of its Revolutionary War prominence. In addition, a great new eastern park will come under the direction of the National Park Service during the coming year — the beautiful Shenandoah Park of Virginia in which C.C.C. men have been working during the past two years.

Two other national parks are that of Hawaii and that of Mt. McKinley in Alaska. The Hawaii park includes the volcanoes of Haleakala, Mauna Loa, and Kilauea, the two last-named being active. Snow-clad Mt. McKinley, rising 20,000 feet above rolling plateaus inhabited by caribou and white mountain sheep, was made a national park principally to protect the magnificent herds of game animals.

State parks, as a systematically planned development, are in their infancy. There are only about 4,500,000 acres of timberland devoted to state park purposes. Of this, the Adirondack State Park of New York state comprises nearly one half — 2,000,000 acres. In 1933–1934, however, nearly 500,000 acres were added to state park lands in thirty-two of the states. Texas, with an increase of nearly 250,000 acres, contributed nearly half of this. Additions to old parks or the creation of new state parks during this period have been made by more than half of the states; namely: New York, Texas, Kentucky, Illinois, Alabama, California, South Carolina, West Virginia, Arkansas, Georgia, Mississippi, North Dakota, North Carolina, Missouri, Minnesota, Oklahoma, Pennsylvania, Iowa, Maryland, New Mexico, Nebraska, Louisiana, Massachusetts, Michigan, New Jersey, Wisconsin, Oregon, and Virginia.

To protect these national forests, national parks, and monuments, and to protect and develop state park lands is the paramount duty of the hundreds of thousands of C.C.C. men now encamped in their midst. Fire and disease destroy national forests and the trees which add so much to the scenic value of national and state parks. Fire can better be controlled in these governmental reservations if there are truck trails and roads into the forests for use by forest fire fighters.

Lookout towers and telephonic communication are essential to such protection. The making of national parks more accessible and more comfortable for visitors is necessary if the greatest benefits are to be gained from them. Work has to be done in the timber lands of the states if the states are to create a forest or park system of their own. This was the major job upon which the men of the C.C.C. were put to work in the spring of 1933. It was into these forests and these national parks that the "Forest Army" was marched, or driven in Army trucks. It was in these forests and parks that thousands of young men from the big cities of the nation got their first sight of the mountains, the lakes, and the big trees.

⋆ 5 ⋆

THE GREAT ADVENTURE

THE "Great Adventure" began amid scenes of revelry and homesickness, fault finding and guitar music. No man of the million who have been in the C.C.C. will forget his first days in "conditioning" camp. Memories of "the needle," or his "ankle chokers," or his first "snipe" hunt will stay with him always. He never will forget the first time he tried to balance a mess kit full of food, his first hot night on woolen G.I. blankets, nor his first contact with an Army sergeant. The mess kit was a mystery, the blankets terrible, and the sergeant no one less than a General. Nor will he forget the tentful of strangers he bunked with that first night in camp, or the misery of homesickness that kept him awake.

Strangers were all around him, hundreds of them. Like himself, they had been selected in the surrounding towns and cities, and gathered in this camp for examination, vaccination, and inoculation; to be outfitted with clothes, organized into a work company, and eventually shipped out to some forest camp. They were men of all sizes and creeds, college men and illiterates, "tough guys" and "softies." But all were Americans who, either for the adventure or through lack of family finances, had signed up for this new conservation army. Here, in conditioning camp, they were to get their first taste of the life they would live for the next six months, if they could stick it out.

Into this vortex of new experience had been drawn many young men of the big cities; men from the towns who never before had been separated from their homes; men from the country, shy and awkward, and not a little awed. All had been caught in the same eddy of unemployment .and were seeking a way out. Some were lured by the thought of free food and clothes and life away from home. Others, held more securely by the sentiments of home life, were motivated by a real desire to help support a struggling family. In their ranks were meek and silent youths; also strident and boastful ones. There were boys from high school and college and from homes of culture. There were men from the slums and the water fronts. Some were ambitious; some, carefree. But for all of them, months in a camp, in the forests or mountains, savored of adventure. All were ready for a new, untried, and thrill-filled life.

There were those thankful for an opportunity of doing something. There were those ready to lead a riot when the meat was tough, the beans scorched, or the coffee cold. There were those who could string tall stories of real and imaginary exploits "on the road" or in the dance hall. And there were those who stole away at night because they could not endure the separation from home, or because they tired of the restricted and ordered life of the camp.

The man who stayed looks back to his days in conditioning camp as crowded, eventful ones which "conditioned" him for many things besides his stay in the woods. He recalls the gradual formation of friendships with the men with whom he was thrown. He recalls with a shudder the fear of the inoculation needle instilled in him by the initiated ones; and he laughs at the terror he threw into others afterwards. There was the day, for instance, when he and his new buddies feigned death after having passed before the doctors, just for the effect it would have on the line of men still waiting to pass before the needle. He recalls changing his "civies" for his first suit of G.I. clothes, and the guffaws that followed. He laughed, too, at pants that would not pull on over his big Army shoes, or would have come nearer fitting the camp water tank. He recalls his first issue of denims and the feel of Army underwear next to his not yet sun-browned back. There was his first "fall out" for camp "policing" — picking up bits of paper and cigaret butts — and the night he was called from his bunk and lined up in the dark with other rookies and told to follow the "officer." There was the morning after, when he and the others were found in a near-by woods, shivering from a night in the open, "waiting for further orders." There was the sheepish feeling he had when marched back to camp by a real officer, who, on discovering half his men missing had thought they had deserted, and then learned that some of the "veterans" had played a prank on the new men. But there was the time, later, when he, as a ten-day "old timer" had taken another rookie into the woods and had instructed him in the art of "snipe" hunting — giving him a bag and posting him beside a log to wait until the "snipe" was chased into his bag, while he went back to his bed and the rookie waited until dawn without sight or sound of "snipe."

He will never forget the "where do we go from here" suspense that hung over the camp from the day he arrived until he left, giving rise to jest and speculation and forming the chief topic of tent conversation. "We're going to Oregon." "No, we're headed for the marsh lands of New Jersey." "The sergeant says he saw an order sending us to Colorado." "All the outfits here are going up to Tennessee." Or: "If they send me near home, I'll quit." "I don't have to stay in this outfit. I signed up just to go to the mountains." "I don't have to work unless I want to." Then the elation, or the dampened spirits, when orders did come to pack up and get ready to move on.

Not until they piled into trucks or filed into railroad coaches did some of the outfits know just where they were going. But go they did — from the conditioning camps into the forests and parks of the country, or along grotesquely eroded hillsides or mosquito-infested waste lands. Many companies of men traveled hundreds of miles to their work camps; some spent days crossing the continent to reach the heavily timbered forest lands and national parks of the West. The men were from the cities and towns of the plains, mostly. Some never had been on a train before, and few had been in the mountains or the big-tree forests. Timber-mantled mountains of the East thrilled them. The rugged peaks of the

Rockies, stretching far above the timber line, struck awe in the men from New York and Chicago. To be able to see a hundred miles away was unbelievable. The splendor of the national parks, Grand Canyon, Zion, Rainier, and the rest, was almost beyond the ken of the men from "the Loop" and "the East Side."

These men were set down at mountainous way stops, to be hauled in trucks up treacherous roads to camp sites. Often it was through rain and mud. More than one truck became mired or tipped over, scattering its load of supplies or equipment. Then the men would get out and push, or trudge on foot over trails yet to be widened into roads by their own hands. Throughout the country young men were on the move — into the cypress growths of the South, into the hardwoods of the lower Appalachians, into the White Mountains and Green Mountains of New England, the Adirondacks and Catskills of New York, the big woods of Michigan, Wisconsin, and Minnesota, and into the Black Hills country of South Dakota and Wyoming, the Rocky Mountains of various states, the Sierra Nevada of California, and the giant fir and pine forests of Washington and Oregon.

The lucky companies found camps established by an advance detail. The others took tents and stoves and food supplies with them. Not a few had to clear away stumps or bowlders before they could unfurl their tents and pin them into place. Rubber boots and duckboards became indispensable. Kitchens were set up with nothing but a tent fly between them and the rain. Cooks and "kitchen police" had to build fires of wet wood in field ranges that did not protect the fire. Straggling lines of bedraggled city youths would file past with mess kits, to eat a supper of simple food and then crawl into blankets to keep warm until another day of mud and rocks and simple food would dawn. These men were the pioneers of the C.C.C. Hundreds of thousands of those who came after them found camps built and barracks ready for them to move into.

But pioneers have their days of despair and anguish. Their spirit sags, and they want to get back where beds are soft and life is less difficult, even if more uncertain. There were many days of despondency among those early ones in the forest work camps. Young men who had been used to movies and dances and baseball games now were isolated in the woods. Food cooked in the open did not always suit their taste, nor was it then of great variety. Cold nights and mornings, without hot water for washing, did not help maintain cheerful dispositions. Money was scarce, and cigarets were smoked to shortest possible butts. Letters from home and girl friends were held up because of the change of location. There were days of desperation. And there were boys who "couldn't take it." They invented excuses to go back home, or walked out without adieu, or provoked officers into discharging them.

Morale began to mount, however, once the camps were built and the men were started on their work in the forests. The men found time to beautify their camps and get acquainted with the others with whom they were eating and sleeping and working. Hours of time were spent landscaping their little towns in the woods, all after their regular hours of labor were over. Trees were set out, flowers were planted, and sidewalks and driveways of stone and sand were stretched along the company "street" between the rows of tents. Artistic stone fountains were constructed, and elaborate stone or rustic arches were built at the entrances to the camps. Decorative fences and the stones were whitewashed, and flag poles were set up Wooden structures for kitchen and mess hall, and for recreational activities, added much to the growing spirit of the men, and they began to settle down to enjoy their new life.

Mail began arriving regularly, and the men began writing letters to their girl friends at home. Some of these letters were the first of their sort these men ever had written. The company clerk or some other of the better-educated men frequently were called upon for a supply of additional words to embellish the letters. Then came payday. With the first money earned in a long time, the men began going to near-by towns, where they could see a movie, flirt with the girls, and buy beer. Those who stayed in camp soon learned the thrill and woes of surreptitious games with "galloping dominoes."

The men also were becoming better acquainted with their officers, and the camp superintendent and foremen under whom they worked.   And the officers and foremen were getting better acquainted with the men. Regular Army officers were in charge of nearly all the first outfits of this new forest army. Some had difficulty in adjusting themselves to the idea that they were commanding civilian groups of men who did not have to salute them, or stand at attention when they entered their tents or barracks.   There were young riots here and there, and some wholesale discharging of "trouble makers." But the great majority of both the Regular Army officers, and the Reserve Corps officers who succeeded them, did understand the men and did much to inspire and console them through trying times. Men began taking their personal troubles to their commanding officer, telling him about difficulties in camp or at home. Officers frequently became the source of a "touch" for a "dime or two bits until payday." Later, when the men were discharged, the officers did much to help them get jobs and "carry on" after getting home. One company commander in Ohio wrote a personal letter to the parents of each boy going home. "Your boy is now on his way home, to be with you from now on," he wrote. "I want you to know that I have enjoyed his stay here, and it is my earnest hope that he will carry on the good work at home just as he has here in camp. He has been obedient, trustworthy, and has learned the value of loyalty and co-operation. May he carry on for you as he has for me."

Another true story illustrates the relationship which grew between the men and the Army officers. A boy from a North Carolina camp had been granted a leave to go home. His home was in the city in which headquarters for the corps area was located. The youth overstayed his leave because of conditions beyond his control, but he did not know just what "the captain" would say when he got back. So he went to corps area headquarters and asked to see the General. The General saw him, heard his story, and invited him to his home for lunch. After lunch the boy and the General had a smoke and the General wrote the magic words on the boy's pass to extend it until he could get back to camp. Then, as the boy was leaving, the General pushed a ten-dollar bill into his hand.

It was not long before the men began to boast of their officers. "We have the best set of officers in the whole C.C.C.," was claimed by almost every camp in the country. Officers and men began to work for the honor of having the best camp in their district or their corps area. And there was much competition for these awards. When the Regular Army officers were called back to their other duties, or when Reserve Corps officers were relieved after having served an allotted time with an outfit, it was difficult to determine whether the officers or the men were more affected by the leaving.

As soon as the camps were near enough to completion to permit proper inhabitation, the men were turned over to the forestry work superintendent and his foremen. They were given axes, saws, picks, shovels, spray guns, and brush hooks, and they began their work in the forests. Divided into work crews, some built roads and trails, others began stringing telephone lines or building drift fences, others cleared forest stands of snags and underbrush. In some camps the main job was that of attacking the moth or the beetle, or checking the spread of blister rust. In the parks there was much roadside clearing and soil erosion work to be done, picnic grounds to be built, and lakes to be cleared. The men were instructed in the purpose of their work, and they were taught how to swing an ax and push a saw. They learned the value of crown and drainage to the life of roads and trails. They saw the need of protecting the forests against fire and replanting those parts which had been burned away.

Work was new to these men. There were many blisters and sore muscles during the early days of their work. But they soon bared their backs to the sun and worked without shirts. Many of them wore nothing but shoes, socks, and G.I. "shorts." Bodies gradually became tanned, and the muscles tough, and the men began to brag about their accomplishments on the job. Loading more truckloads of earth or gravel than any other crew, or clearing more miles of firebreak, or stretching more telephone line, were usual grounds of controversy. Along with their discussion of girls and government, this became the center of conversation between work time and bed time. Some men drove trucks. Others operated tractors and "bulldozer" road machines. Some became members of the dynamite crew and others helpers to the engineers.

When work progressed to great distances from camp, side-camps were established. Twelve or more men would live there by themselves, usually under direction of a foreman, and work in the immediate vicinity. Here the men got deeper into the wilds of the country and lived under conditions more primitive than in the main camp. Often, in order to get time enough off to spend a week-end at the main camp, or in town, these men would work ten and twelve hours a day until they got in their required hours of work for the week, and then have an extra day to make the trip down the mountain. Sometimes a day of rain would come. There would be no work, and the men would have to stay in over the week-end to make up the lost time. Men were required to work 40 hours each week. Time lost because of rain had to be made up.

It was both on the job and in camp that the shirkers and the "tired" were discovered, by officers, foremen, and the other men. The men gave them a name. "Goldbrickers," they called them. And many camp commanders or work superintendents made up special crews of these "goldbrickers" and delegated to them the more distasteful jobs about camp. Other men, because of their willingness to work, their especial aptitudes, or their ability to direct others, were given promotions from the "ranks." They became Leaders and Assistant Leaders. Those positions corresponded somewhat to those of the corporal and the sergeant in the Army, and brought the men more pay — $45 per month for the Leaders and $36 per month for the Assistant Leaders. One of the Leaders was a Senior Leader. He was the boss of the camp, under the Army officers. His job was to see that the men got to work, that they obeyed disciplinary regulations, that the camp was in proper order, that the cooks were supplied with "K.P.'s," to peel potatoes and scrub pans, and do sundry other tasks of a similar nature. Other Leaders included cooks, office clerks, first-aid men, supply clerks, work crew bosses, and assistants to educational advisers. Many of these latter have been promoted to positions of forestry foremen upon leaving the C.C.C. Provisions now allow the retention of these Leaders who wish to remain in the C.C.C. after the usual maximum term of service has expired. When new companies are organized many of these men form the nucleus around which the recruits are organized.

Men cannot live in the forests or the mountains without either falling under their spell or being frightened into deserting. The mountains and the big trees do something to man. The stillness of the mountains at night did something to the men of the C.C.C. So did the grandeur of the peaks at sunrise or at sunset. Walled in by the mountains or great stretches of pine or spruce, the men could not help feeling their immensity, and the unimportance and smallness of themselves in comparison. There were men from the North in Tennessee and Florida, men from Texas in Colorado, men from New Jersey in Idaho, men from along the Mississippi up in the woods of the North. Swimming in mountain lakes, fishing for trout, and scaling the mountains was new sport for them. So was skiing, snowshoeing and tobogganing for the men stationed in Maine, New York, and Michigan and the West. Exploring old gold mines and panning gold from the streams became popular. So did classes in botany and forestry, under direction of camp foresters or park naturalists.

The men began to study birds and animals. Hardly a camp in the country has not had from one to a dozen pets from the forests as "mascots." The most popular has been the black bear. From the first night that such bears came around, attracted by the scent of food, the men and the big black bears have been friends. Injured fawns have been found in the woods and brought into camp to be given first aid or fed from a bottle, and held until they were old enough or strong enough to "go it alone" in the forests. Perhaps the most exciting and at the same time most dangerous encounters with wild life have been with snakes. Poisonous reptiles abounded in and near

many of the camp sites. Men early were cautioned against
this danger, and instructed in methods of first aid in case they
were bitten. Some have been bitten, but there have been few
deaths from this cause. Thousands of "rattlers" have met
their doom at the hands of adventurous C.C.C. boys.

Trees, perhaps, have had a greater effect on the sensibili-
ties of the men than any other part of nature. Here are two
bits of verse, one written by a man in a camp in Arkansas;
the other by a man in a camp in Pennsylvania:

PLEASE, OH LORD

Lord, — if you should take away the trees,
  Should deem it wise to economize
On flowers, birds, and bees,
  Should think it best that nature rest,
And have the sun and moon and stars
  Shine only half the time;
If you think it best all this loveliness
  Of Nature should resign,
Then surely we'd have cause to be
  A discontented Nation, at your shrine.

TREES — AN IRREVERENT PARODY

(APOLOGIES TO J. K.)

I must confess that I can't see
Why poets rave about the tree.

They call its roots "its hungry mouth"
(I wish they'd try to dig 'em out).

Those "leafy arms that lift to pray,"
(I've cut 'em day by weary day).

Of course, there's "nests of robins there."
(But who wants robins in their hair?)

They "live with rain," but who has not,
(Who sleeps upon an Army cot?).

Yes, "poems are made by fools like me,"
(But any nut can plant a tree).

But after one has lived in the woods for an extended time, he wants to see "the bright lights," even though they be the lights of a small country village, or just the lights of passing autos on the highway the other side of the mountain. The men of the C.C.C. soon became familiar figures on the streets of the towns nearest the camps. In some places they were not looked upon with much favor at first. They were considered "riffraff," or "charity seekers," or "city boys having a good time in the woods at government expense." But after the communities became acquainted with the work they were doing, and after they became acquainted with the boys themselves, their attitude toward them changed. When the townsfolk learned that "the C.C.C. camp" was making a park for them in "that piece of forest beyond Tyler's place," they began to take an interest in the men who came to town on weekends. After some of the town leaders had been invited out to camp and had eaten with the officers and men, and had sat in on some of their boxing matches or shows, they changed their minds about the C.C.C. being an organization of "bums." They went back home and planned recreation rooms for the boys while visiting town. The churches and the civic and women's organizations then wanted to do things for them. When the merchants discovered that the boys spent many nickels for Hamburg sandwiches, movies, beer, and souvenirs to send home, they became more kindly disposed toward the men in the ill-fitting O.D. clothes that had been remodeled from Army uniforms.

It was not long before the men were being invited into the homes of the village for Sunday dinner and taking the daughters of the house to the movies. Soon the camp ball team was playing the town's team, and the men of "the C.C.C. camp" were participating in town celebrations, taking part in their parades, and acting as guards at their public functions. Nor was it long before the townsfolk were flocking to the camp on Sundays, and hinting for invitations to the camp parties. Occasionally the town constable or sheriff would "entertain" the boys. But this was seldom. The men were on their good behavior while in town, and a slip from discipline meant con-

finement to camp on other week-ends. The police record for
the C.C.C. has been small in comparison with its size. The
communities near which the majority of the camps were located are loud in their praise of the men who made up its
ranks. Company officers have done much to cement this feeling of friendship. The governor of Idaho, commenting upon
the men of the C.C.C., is reported to have said: "These are
the type of men we want in our state. I hope many of' them
will remain here, marry our girls, and raise Idaho potatoes."
Some of the men took the governor at his word. Many of
the C.C.C. men everywhere have married girls in the communities surrounding the camps, even though marriage made
them ineligible for re-enrollment in the C.C.C.

All of this had done much to increase the morale of the men
in the camps. They became camp- and C.C.C.-conscious.
They began to feel themselves as part of an important group
of young men; taking part in a great cause. They desired
to excel in their work and in initiative. The spirit grew up
around both men and officers. The value of each camp soon
could be measured by the interest the officers were taking in
their camp and their men, and the interest the men were taking in their work and their officers. There were men who
looked upon their camps as "just a place to stay," getting
along with as little work as possible. There were officers and
superintendents who have had to be relieved of their camp
commands because they "couldn't make a go of it." But they
are not average men or average officers and superintendents.
The average are those who have built great camps from wild
and rugged camp sites; have done long days of good work
in the forests; have beautified their camps until many of them
are show places of the community in which they are located;
have named their camps after President Roosevelt, Director
Fechner,. Secretary-of-War Dern, Army officers, camp superintendents, men who have died while in camp, or town digni-
taries, or after the mountains, forests, or streams in which or
near which they are located; are proud of their athletic teams
and their work; razz the new "rookies" who are brought in, but
also instruct them in the history and ideals of the camp.

There are approximately 35,000 war veterans in C.C.C. camps. They have been organized into companies of their own and are at work in almost every part of the country. It was difficult for them to enter into the spirit of this new army of young men. They had, for the most part, become disillusioned through lack of employment. But soon the same morale which took them to France during the World War, became evident in the camps. They were older by many years than they were in 1917, but some of the Veterans' organizations are among the outstanding ones in the C.C.C. Most of them are married men, and are supporting a family on the $30 they get from their work each month. Those who are not married are given a small portion of their allowances each payday and the rest is held for them until their enrollment is completed. The same spirit is manifest in the companies of Negroes, many of which are located in the East and South.

It is when the time comes for the men to leave the C.C.C., either because they have "served the limit" or because they want to seek permanent employment, that their attachment to the camp is most marked. Some men leave after having served their original six-months enrollment. Some have promise of work outside, or want to seek it. Some do not find the life and work of the C.C.C. to their liking. More than two thirds of the men, however, stay for the limit of service. All has not been perfect in camp. But, taken all together, it has been a great experience. There are tears in the eyes of many men when they climb into trucks to be taken back to the railroad station for their trip home. There are tears, also, in the eyes of many men who stay behind. There have been farewell banquets for the men, at which officers and men have told each other what "great guys" each thinks the others are. The men have seen the mountains and the forests and it has been a great experience.

But each man has left behind him a monument. It may stretch up and down and around a mountain, in the form of a broad fire break, it may be a new forest road or trail, it may be a dam to protect the land from floods — but it is evidence of his contribution to the forests or the fields of the land.

HOLDI

* 6 *

ON FIRE LINE AND TRAIL

FIRE is the great enemy of man in the forests. Protection against fire, and the suppression of fire, are necessary if man is to gain or maintain his control over the natural resources bound up in our vast forest lands. Millions of trees that form this immense reservoir of potential human well-being, and have consumed years in their growth, are destroyed annually because of the inadequate precautionary defenses set up to protect them. The economic loss runs into millions of dollars. And it is man, not nature, who gives most assistance to his worst enemy. Man-caused fires in the forests have outnumbered those attributed to lightning or initiated by other forces.

It is almost as difficult to prevent fires caused by human carelessness, cupidity, or spite as it is to anticipate the places in a forest where lightning will strike or where sparks from a locomotive will start a blaze. Defense is necessary. Fire-fighting offense is a last-stand maneuver. Fortifications — fire breaks, trails and roads, lookout towers, telephone lines, reduced fire hazards — are essential. To build and preserve these lines of defense takes men and money. There has been an insufficient supply of both. Trails and breaks have been stretched for length, rather than for enduring avenues of protection. Available man power has been utilized at times of crisis, when fire has raced over insecure ramparts and threatened annihilation.

There was need of enough fortifying work to keep hundreds of thousands of men employed for several years when the C.C.C. went into the forests in the spring and summer of

1933. There were fire breaks to be cleared and extended, and new ones to be cut; truck trails and roads to be rebuilt and many new ones constructed; snags and underbrush to be reduced from the tinder it had become; towers to be erected and communicating lines established. The C.C.C. men were new at the job, but they soon learned how to handle a shovel and a pick on the roads, the proper way to fell a snag, how to string a telephone line to the trees, and how to haul supplies to a mountain top to build a lookout tower.

As the months passed, with experience that hardened their muscles and gave them a keener eye, the men began to make their presence in the forests count — in thousands of miles of trails and roads, and wide ribbons of open fire break. Down through New England, New York, and Pennsylvania they stretched, and into the mountains of Virginia, the Carolinas, Georgia, and Florida. Up through the Middle West, and into the woods of the North new fronts of defense were thrown up, zigzagging across the forests and parks. In the mountains of Wyoming, Colorado, and New Mexico hundreds of thousands of acres of timber were given a chance to grow without constant fear of feeling the breath of flames at their boles or their crowns. Into the great softwoods of Washington, Oregon, and California, and through the heavy timber lands of Idaho, Montana, and Utah; into the Big Tree country of the Sierras and the parks of Arizona, men from New York and Chicago, Seattle and Spokane, San Francisco and Los Angeles were opening breaks and trails that are as columns of troops or long batteries of artillery in a battle of the forests. Even in Hawaii, Alaska, Puerto Rico, and the Virgin Islands forests were given a better chance to grow and greater prospect of reaching maturity.

But this is only part of the work done by these young foresters. Fires came while the men were in the woods — 1934 was one of the most hazardous forest-fire years. Great fires raged through the mountains of the West, in California, Oregon, Washington, Idaho, and Montana. Hardly a state escaped without its fire losses; scarcely a C.C.C. camp went through the summer without its fire-fighting experience. The men have spent over 1,600,000 man-days fighting forest fires. They have done gallant service. Several lost their lives during the big fires of the West; many accounts of heroic deeds came back from the fire lines where, at times, men fought for days and nights with little rest between, to subdue this smoke-bellowing enemy of the forests. An indication of the work done by the C.C.C. in the forests is gained from the records which show that forest-fire losses in 1934 were reduced by 17 per cent in the national forests and by 35 per cent in the national parks, from the average annual fire loss of the preceding five years.

Insidious fellow-enemies of the forests, yet in no league with forest fire, are the blights and insects that choke the life of forest trees quite as effectively as fire burns it out. Chief among these enemies are blister rust, the gypsy moth, and Dutch elm blight.

Blister rust, brought here from Europe, as are most of the blights which are fatal to American trees, was making a heavy inroad into our white pines. It propagates and is disseminated through currant and gooseberry bushes. The spore is wafted from infected tree to bush, and from bush to healthy tree. Several thousand C.C.C. men have devoted the greater share of their time to the eradication of these ribes. Idaho, particularly, has been a battle front on which this war has been waged, in an effort to check the spread of the blight through the soft pine country of the Far Northwest. The currant and gooseberry bushes have been pulled or sprayed on hundreds of thousands of acres throughout the country since the spring of 1933.

The gypsy moth, introduced into this country, so the story says, by a Frenchman who had hopes of mating it with the silkworm, to create a more hardy silk producer, has spread throughout all of New England, down into New York and New Jersey, and has jumped the Hudson River, on its way into the oaks of the Middle West. A "no-moths' land" now extends from the outskirts of New York City to the Canadian border, in which C.C.C. outfits are endeavoring to drive the moth back east into the Atlantic Ocean. Moth control squads have been working for two years in the New England states, hunting out the eggs and destroying them with creosote. Thousands of acres of land have been covered, particularly in Massachusetts, Connecticut, Rhode Island, and Maine, in the attempt to eradicate this insect.

Dutch elm disease is, as its name implies, a blight that creeps into the elm tree through its leaves, reaching the body and "strangling" it. This infestation is centered around New York City and New Jersey, but its spread into the great elms of upper New York and Ohio is threatened. Many owners of prized elms will be grateful to the C.C.C. for their work in combating the Dutch elm blight.

And now the ditch digging. For it takes almost every variety of labor, from working in the mud to archæological research, to make the beauty of the national parks and monuments stand out in all their natural splendor. It is not a matter of "gilding the lily," but of "dressing to best display one's charms." Besides protecting the forests in the park and monument areas from the ravages of fire, there is much work to be done to best display the charms with which nature has endowed this part of the globe we call America. Roadsides need to be cleared of the débris that mars the beauties that surround them. Foot and horse trails need to be made passable and located so as to afford the hiker and the rider the most advantageous views of scenery or the most impressive retreats into nature's seclusion. Parks, to give the visitor the most for his efforts to reach them, must offer him a place to camp and pure water to drink. Trees and plants must be guarded against disease, banks of streams and rivers must be maintained, and foot bridges and benches and guard rails must be provided. This sort of work has been the job of the C.C.C. during the past two years. More than 25,000 miles of park roads and trails made more beautiful show the results of their labor. More than 60,000 miles of water supply system installation also add to the evidence of the long list of improvements which are helping our national parks and monuments to become more accessible and their radiance more alluring. Nothing approaching the scope of this work ever has been undertaken by any other government. Through it the nation's recreational areas already have been advanced further than would have been possible in ten or twenty years under the "old order." These conservation activities take the form of landscape protection, and the work is conducted with detailed attention to the landscape values rather than to those of timber values. Forest areas in the parks are kept in their natural condition as much as possible. The removal of underbrush, dead trees, and other natural débris is undertaken only to such an extent as to remove serious fire hazards. Ground protection is essential in the propagation of bird life and small animals, and also is part of the natural forest scene. Landscape engineers prescribe the manner of work done in the parks.

The same type of work is being done at many of the national monuments under supervision of the National Park Service, and in the many historical and military parks, and on battlefield sites. From the restoration of Old Fort Pulaski, on an island in the Savannah River, in Georgia, where C.C.C. men are reclaiming the brick structures and ancient parade ground from the mud, to Death Valley National Memorial, where fresh water springs are being located at advantageous spots along a new oil-coated wagon trail, for the convenience of tourists to heretofore almost inaccessible parts, the C.C.C. is making long strides in pushing our national park and monument system into realms of reality only dreamed of before 1933. More than 500 companies, of 200 men each, are under the direction of the National Park Service and other allied agencies of the Department of the Interior, which plans the work the men do and supervises them on the job.

Of these more than 500 groups of young workers, 348 are located on projects in state parks. These parks have been given great impetus through Emergency Conservation Work. There were few states that did not have under-developed parks, or lands suitable for making new parks. When plans were made to send the C.C.C. into the forests and parks of the country the governors of the various states were invited to participate in the program. New state parks now are being

developed, or existing ones enlarged or given a "houseclean-
ing" by men of the C.C.C. in forty-one of the states. Many
of these states — particularly Virginia, West Virginia, South
Carolina, Mississippi, and New Mexico — are making their
first ventures into state park development. Lands for these
have been acquired by either gift or purchase. Other states
are pondering legislation to provide for similar use of their
available beauty spots and historic monuments. Forty per
cent of the work projects in Texas, for instance, are of state
park nature. Texas has increased her state park properties
by a quarter of a million acres during the past two years.
California has added seven new state parks in the same time,
and has increased the size of six old ones by some 28,000 acres.
Virginia has taken in 15,000 acres and Oklahoma 13,000,
each in a single park. In Iowa men are working on forty-five
state park projects.

The 75,000 men who are at work in these parks throughout the country are improving the timber tracts, helping to
save the topography from erosion and floods, clearing up camp
grounds and picnic areas, building foot, horse, and vehicle
trails, bridges, shelters, picnic tables and fireplaces, and
developing swimming, boating, and fishing facilities. Some
of the state park projects, however, are among the most extensive being carried on by Emergency Conservation Work.
At Skokie Lagoons Park, near Chicago, 2,000 men are engaged reclaiming from swamp lands what eventually will be
one of the largest public recreation spots of the country.
More than 2,000 men are working in various parts of Palisades
State Park in New York state. A thousand men are encamped
adjacent to Milwaukee, one of the projects being that of building, on the shores of Lake Michigan at Sheridan Military
Park, a bathing beach that involves the construction of concrete jetties, 200 and 300 feet long — building the concrete
blocks that go into them and erecting the jetties in four and
five feet of water. Bathing suits and high "waders" are part
of the equipment of these men. Other outstanding state
projects are those at Natural Bridge and Cumberland Falls,
Kentucky; at old Fort Frederick in Maryland; at Boulder

Dam, Nevada; Camden, New Jersey; Roosevelt state park in North Dakota, where 600 men are stationed; the Schoenbrunn Memorial Park in Ohio, which work is being done by a war veterans' outfit; the Tennessee Valley projects, in Tennessee and Alabama, where nine of the twenty-eight T.V.A. companies are engaged principally in state park work; the Custer State Park in South Dakota, with 800 men; in Virginia, where 3,000 men are engaged in various developments under state park supervision; at Guernsey Lake, Wyoming; and at the Deception Pass and Millersylvania projects in Washington.

One of the major designs of Emergency Conservation Work is that of forestation, reforestation, and vegetation. Planting millions of trees where trees have not grown for many years or where more recently they have been burned away, has occupied the "eight hour a day, five days a week" of many thousands of the men since the early months of the C.C.C. They are giving a new, verdant life to lands abandoned after lumbering operations to grow up in "scrub;" lands that have been burned over, once or many times; lands which have reverted from farm acreage and have been purchased by the state or nation for forests or parks; rolling sections or prairie lands that have been impoverished by countless grass fires; eroded hillsides that have become the "bad lands" of many states; and forest lands depleted by disease. These broad stretches of country are being planted or have been planted with millions of young pines and locust seedlings and trees of other varieties. Wisconsin and Michigan lead in reforestation. These states, once "forests primeval," later forced to import lumber for their own use, are illustrative of exploitive lumber cutting. A million and a half acres of land have recently been purchased by the federal government in Wisconsin, to be added to national forests. More than 30,-000,000 trees have been planted in Wisconsin by the C.C.C. Almost an equal number, 28,000,000, have been added to forest lands of Michigan. Large areas in New York have been reforested with 15,000,000, and large areas in Minnesota with 12,500,000; and Indiana has 19,000,000 young black locust trees growing, mostly in an effort to check erosion.

Each state has had its own fields of "waste" lands that are among the millions of acres of potential forest area of the country.

Forestation by the C.C.C., however, caught the forest nurseries unprepared for such a gigantic undertaking. Consequently, many outfits of C.C.C. men have become "nurserymen." Nurseries had to be enlarged and others had to be established. The C.C.C. was moved in and told how to go about it. Such large federal nurseries as those at Jackson, Tennessee, the Rhinelander nurseries in Wisconsin, and the Catahoula nursery in Louisiana have become "wartime munition plants" in their effort to keep seedlings available for necessary planting. These nurseries have capacities of from ten to twenty millions of young trees. Land was leased in Indiana for the establishment of thirteen nurseries for the growing of the black locust; 35,000,000 plants have got their start there so far. Nurseries in Montana and Washington, operated with C.C.C. help, have been supplying a great part of the demand in the Far Northwest. Other men, in North Dakota camps, are engaged in experimental work which will aid in determining the most suitable species of trees for planting in the 1,000-mile forest-shelter belt, to be constructed through the Great Plains states from Canada to the Texas Panhandle. Many varieties of pine, spruce, and cedar are being "tested" in the soil and climate of the region. Many of the 4,000 men of the C.C.C. located in the T.V.A. section of the South are engaged in landscaping and reforestation with the seedlings raised by other C.C.C. men in the many nurseries conducted by the U. S. Forest Service, the National Park Service, and the states.

Seed, too, was scarce when the C.C.C. went into the forests, and many of the men were sent out to gather it. Millions of pounds of seed were collected and turned over to the nurseries for growing. Other men have spent a large portion of their time on the ranges in the west, in an effort to afford them revegetation to replace the wasted fields on which no animal can live to its full weight and age. Another more or less allied work of the C.C.C. has been that of assisting in the timber stand survey being conducted by the U. S. Forest Service. This is the largest survey of its kind ever made and is to determine the variety and quality of timber stands, the rate of growth, the tendency to reproduction, and other valuable information.

But timber cannot grow, nor parks remain beautiful, if the rain and the wind carry away the top soil and wash it down through gullies and into streams. This is one reason why soil erosion control has played a large part in the work program of the C.C.C. Lands not cared for fall prey to the wear and tear and waste of erosion. Gullies, wide and deep, eat their way into the land, bringing down trees and soil as they eat. To check the extensive gnawing of these gullies is an important job of the C.C.C. In the forests, in the parks, and on stream-improvement projects the men have constructed more than a million check dams of brush and timber and stone across the avaricious mouths of these gullies, and planted them with trees. In some sections of the country they have worked in co-operation with groups of farmers to assist them in halting the disastrous effects of erosion. Fifty thousand men have been employed in this manner and have made a large advance toward controlling erosion in many states. They work under the direction of the soil erosion services of the Department of Agriculture and the Department of the Interior, 148 companies with the former and 51 with the latter. In Mississippi, alone, there have been 27 camps of men engaged in this form of conservation, six of them on private erosion projects. They have built nearly 200,000 small check dams. This, likewise, has been a chief "objective" up through Tennessee, Kentucky, Ohio, and Indiana.

Perhaps the most extensive operations of this nature have been carried on through the Plains states, from Iowa and Nebraska down into Texas. Nearly 4,000 men have been building dams, digging ditches, and protecting the banks against erosion in Iowa, 1,800 in Missouri, and several hundred in Nebraska. In Oklahoma and Texas, the greater part of the work has been in conjunction with farm owners in the affected regions. Here, ever since their last harvest, these farmers have been working alongside C.C.C. outfits. The land owners perform terracing operations on their respective properties and the C.C.C. men build permanent dams to protect terrace outlets and plant the gullies with trees. Terracing includes the construction of shallow, wide ditches around the hillsides at right angles to the encroaching gullies. These empty into the master outlets constructed by the 3,000 men working in this two-state territory. In several other Middle Western states studies and surveys have been made of needs for terracing work, and agreements have been signed with the landowners of large acreages who agree to terrace their properties in order to obtain camp assistance in their erosion control problems.

The extent of man's dependence on nature for economic life and for esthetic life as well is illustrated in the multifarious, "close to the soil" work that has occupied C.C.C. men from the beginning. The tabulation of work accomplishments, on pages 77–79, indicates the variety of labor, and the amount accomplished during the first eighteen months of Emergency Conservation Work. It includes much that has been done in flood control work, especially that accomplished in Vermont, where 4,000 men, all war veterans, worked for a year and a half in the Winooski River valley, under direction of Army engineers, to help reduce the menace of floods which had brought destruction and death to the valley several times during the preceding few years. It includes similar work on the levees along the lower Mississippi River, and extensive projects in Kansas. Mosquito control work also is recorded, the outstanding project being that in Delaware, where the state and Emergency Conservation Work are laboring in common, draining swamp land and making it taboo for the mosquito that has emigrated from the "Jersey" marshes. Work of the Biological Survey, of the Department of Agriculture, also is noted — important work in which hundreds of men are engaged, developing sanctuaries for birds, game, and fish. Other work is shown for the project at Beltsville, Maryland, where two companies of C.C.C. workers are improving a 4,000-acre experimental farm maintained by the federal government.   It tells of aviation fields built, of narrow-gauge railroad construction, of searching for missing persons, which has taken many man-days and has been most successful, and of fighting long-standing fire in coal mines in Wyoming. It does not mention, specifically, the American Indians who are established in camps on their own reservations, doing the same sort of work the other men are doing, but under the direction of the Bureau of Indian Affairs, of the Department of the Interior.   There are 14,000 of these Indians at work — some live at home and walk to the job, others move their families into camp on the project.   They are at work on 53 reservations distributed through the country, reclaiming their own lands from erosion, fire, and the lack of water for their cattle. Emergency Conservation Work is giving the Indians of the reservations a new lease on life that at times is dry, difficult, and spiritless on heat-blown prairies or semidesert land.

Such is the work the men from the cities faced when they came into the forests, knowing little of work and almost nothing of the forests or the great areas of eroded or flood-swept lands.   And it was from a day on the roads, or the fire line, the dam project, or the mosquito marshes that they were taken back to camp in the late afternoon, with plenty to do between then and the call for work the next morning.

WORK DONE IN THE FIRST 18 MONTHS OF EMERGENCY CONSERVATION WORK

TYPE OF JOB	UNIT OF MEASURE-MENT	NEW CONSTRUC-TION	MAIN-TENANCE
Telephone lines	Miles	25,089	33,206
Fire breaks	Miles	27,898	11,936
Reduction of fire hazards	Acres	825,808	97
Roadside clearing or clean-up, fire prevention	Miles	17,042	543
Trailside clearing or clean-up, fire prevention	Miles	5,305	288
Lookout houses	Number	487	130
Lookout towers	Number	797	383
Fighting forest fires	Man-days	1,605,326	...
Fire presuppression	Man-days	557,779	...
Fire prevention	Man-days	87,067	64
General clean-up other than fire prevention	Acres	80,142	3,801
Forest stand improvement	Acres	1,392,827	1,623
Roads — (a) Truck trails	Miles	41,582	49,233
(b) Minor	Miles	1,079	8,343
(c) Highway	Miles	268	2,631
Trails — (a) Horse	Miles	5,234	16,598
(b) Foot	Miles	4,162	5,750
Driveways for livestock	Miles	542	282
Dwellings at permanent stations	Number	677	598
Dwellings at temporary or seasonal stations	Number	772	299
Tool houses and boxes	Number	6,909	402
Barns	Number	526	154
Office buildings	Number	528	185
Public camp ground clearing	Acres	22,296	1,124
Public camp ground buildings	Number	1,984	329
Public camp ground latrines	Number	3,355	245
Public camp ground water systems — (a)	Feet	364,672	2,980
(b)	Number	754	28
Public camp ground waste disposal — (a)	Feet	196,647	2,113
(b)	Number	2,068	123
Other public camp ground facilities	Number	30,177	3,802
Other structures	Number	7,554	887
Fences, other than range	Miles	1,985	290
Fences, range	Miles	4,804	1,465
Water systems — (a) Storage facilities	1,000 gals.	94,085	58
(b) Pipe lines	Feet	1,320,707	94,663
(c) Wells and water holes	Number	3,048	218
Spring or well development for livestock or wild life	Number	2,590	36
Reservoirs, water for livestock or wild life	Number	1,874	73
Planting — (a) Forestation	Acres	204,339	6,114
(b) Grasses or grains	Acres	239	...
Nursery	Man-days	392,280	57,114
Experimental plots	Number	5,940	175
Range vegetation	Acres	19,641	753
Seed collection — (a) Conifers (cones)	Bushels	68,165	...
(b) Hardwoods and other	Pounds	360,529	...
(c) Grasses and herbs	Pounds	500	...
Insect pest control — (a) Tree	Acres	2,922,717	6,890
(b) Other	Acres	497,504	...
Rodent control	Acres	9,672,782	34,832

(continued on pp. 78–79)

Type of Job	Unit of Measurement	New Construction	Maintenance
Elimination of — (a) Useless range stock ..	Number	57,132	...
(b) Predatory animals ...	Number	86	..
Tree and plant disease control	Acres	2,657,779	23,267
Eradication of poisonous and other plants.	Acres	121,497	960
Survey — (a) Linear	Miles	49,424	1,346
(b) Topographic	Acres	2,537,109	...
(c) Timber estimating, forest type, range special use, etc.	Acres	12,191,482	60,000
(d) Model or relief maps	Sq. ft.	18,945	...
Ground water surveys	Acres	894,518	...
Eroison control (includes sloping and planting) (a) Dams	Number	778,462	26,863
(b) Land benefited	Acres	1,205,330	18,026
(c) Bank protection (including stream, road, or any other bank)	Sq. yd.	68,824,741	5,158,740
(d) Ditches (drainage, diversion, etc.)	Lin. yd.	419,835	135,791
(e) Fill banks and bared slopes	Acres	1,638	...
(f) Débris barriers	Cu. yd.	9,022	66
(g) Wells, investigated or dug	Number	289	...
(h) Planting, for bank protection	Lin. ft.	1,602,827	16,920
Bridges — (a) Foot	Number	3,087	30
(b) Horse	Number	635	41
(c) Vehicle	Number	18,595	1,912
(d) Stock; also cattle guards and gates	Number	1,255	59
Water improvement — (a) Lake, pond, or beach	Acres	30,647	...
(b) Stream	Miles	5,049	48
(c) Restocking fish .	Number	5,896,610	20,000
(d) Planting for water fowl	Acres	40	...
Ponds for fish and birds	Number	2,094	337
Dams, recreational	Number	1,041	33
Corrals	Number	306	28
Flood control —			
(a) Surveys — Line and grade	Lin. ft.	17,201,440	6,158
(b) Topographic	Sq. yd.	94,267,569	...
(c) Clearing — Dam site	Sq. yd.	3,832,824	...
(d) River bank	Sq. yd.	18,946,308	...
(e) Channel	Lin. yd.	324,318	...
(f) Dams — Earth fill	Cu. yd.	3,404,124	40,183
(g) Stripping of site	Cu. yd.	152,164	...
(h) Earth excavation	Cu. yd.	491,849	...
(i) Rock excavation	Cu. yd.	103,312	...
(j) Concrete	Cu. yd.	51,335	255
(k) Rock fill	Cu. yd.	375,128	1,162
(l) Steel	Pounds	1,233,031	...
(m) Channel { Earth excavation	Cu. yd.	372,649	750
(n) enlargement { Rock excavation	Cu. yd.	93,558	90
(o) Rock excavation	Cu. yd.	36,414	...
(p) Reconstruc- Earth excavation	Cu. yd.	14,150	...
(q) tion of ex- Concrete removal	Cu. yd.	157	...
(r) isting dams New concrete	Cu. yd.	2,175	2,355
(s) Steel	Pounds	188,000	...

TYPE OF JOB	UNIT OF MEASURE-MENT	NEW CONSTRUC-TION	MAIN-TENANCE
(*t*) Levees	Cu. yd.	490,245	703
(*u*) Cribbing, includes riprap filling	Lin. ft.	271,724	214
(*v*) Water-spreading dikes	Lin. ft.	15,282	...
(*w*) Water-spreading dikes	Cu. yd.	1,404	...
(*x*) Dams, rubble masonry	Cu. yd.	14,721	480
Landscaping —			
(*a*) Undifferentiated	Acres	27,634	172
(*b*) Fine grading (road slopes, parking areas, etc.)	Cu. yd.	290,821	50
(*c*) Soil preparation	Sq. yd.	409,739	...
(*d*) Seeding or sodding	Acres	369	13
(*e*) Moving and planting trees or shrubs	Number	154,037	77,223
(*f*) Tree surgery	Man-days	11,184	104
Landing fields, airplanes — (*a*)	Acres	2,910	240
(*b*)	Number	6	1
Fighting coal fires	Man-shift	24,766	...
Guard rails — (*a*) Undifferentiated	Miles	2,773	...
(*b*) Timber	Lin. ft.	34,876	...
(*c*) Masonry	Cu. yd.	891	...
Searching for missing persons	Man-days	8,740	...
Mosquito control — (*a*) Ditching	Lin. yd.	1,369,114	500,890
(*b*) Staking	Lin. yd.	805,054	...
(*c*) Spraying	Man-days	...	4,558
Narrow gauge railroad	Acres	400	...
Narrow gauge railroad	Miles	10	...

"DARLIN' NELLIE GRAY"   80   "MOUNTAIN CHARM"

★ 7 ★

"LIFE" BEGINS AT 4:30 P.M.

THE "Life" of a C.C.C. camp begins at 4:30 — when the men pile from the trucks which have brought them back from their eight hours of work on the project. From then until "lights out," usually at ten o'clock, there is much to occupy their time and energies. They are allowed to follow their own inclinations, in keeping with camp disciplinary restrictions. Their "diversions" include mess at 5 o'clock, which, without exception, is placed at the head of each man's list of selections. Among other possible choices are practically every form of athletic and social life of which any well-appointed town can boast. The rules which have to be obeyed include such as going to town only with permission, maintaining camp property, and observing order.

Some camps are conducted on a self-government plan. Others are ruled by two-fisted Army officers who go the limit permitted by the book of regulations. A few camps suffer from laxity of proper control. In almost every camp there is an organization of men who plan and recommend measures for camp betterment. In some, they are charged with the task of assisting in the enforcement of camp discipline. These groups generally are made up of the camp Leaders, with company officers and camp superintendent sitting in their meetings. These men bring in suggestions from the rank and file of the outfit, advise ways and means of making the camp a better place in which to live, and consider the problems which arise while the men are at work. Officers and work superintendents depend to no small degree upon these men to keep the camp and the job functioning properly.

Some companies have formed their camps into "towns." Formal elections are held for mayor, chief of police, judges, and council. Even the party system is in vogue, and the men hold fastidiously to parliamentary procedure in the conduct of their meetings and their trials. Violations of camp rules are, in many instances, turned over to such camp governments, and their "laws" and court decisions are binding unless vetoed or overruled by the C.O. A man may be placed on trial for coming in late and overturning a bunk after its occupant has gone to sleep. He is permitted a defense attorney, is accused by "the camp" and as many witnesses as are available and will testify. His case is considered either by a jury of his campmates or by the judge. Penalty may be a fine or a restriction to camp for a definite time. Such fines go into the company fund used for the benefit of the entire camp. The men learn much from such court practice and become more interested in the maintenance of the camp.

Dances and parties in camp became popular after the wooden recreation halls were erected, and after the men became acquainted in the community. Some C.C.C. camps are the social center of the entire countryside. Crepe paper and bits of nature's green transform these barracks into ballrooms on such occasions. The parties usually are held on Friday nights because Saturday is not a work day — unless there is time to be made up for idleness caused by rain during the week. Fancy steps and old-fashioned square dances are tripped off to the tunes of the latest Broadway hits or of mountain folk songs. Girls are brought in from the surrounding towns. Some of them are transported 40 or 50 miles in camp trucks, and then taken home in the same manner. Camp dances are popular with the young women, and they vie with each other for the opportunity of attending them. Wives of Army officers or of foresters, or mothers of some of the girls do the chaperoning. Refreshments of cider and doughnuts, or sandwiches and coffee, usually are served, financed by the men or from company funds. Many of the men had to learn the art of dancing after getting to camp.

Afternoon classes in dancing frequently are held by the men, and it is common to see one man instructing another in the steps of a waltz in the barracks, their heavy Army shoes notwithstanding. Groups of interested townsfolk also have taken over the job of teaching the men of some camps to dance. It has become the "project" of several Junior League groups of the small towns. Wives of the officers play an important part in the social life of some camps, helping the men plan their functions and doing such work as making curtains for the windows of the barracks. Some of the men have met their first girl at camp parties, and it is not uncommon to see officers and foresters and enrollees competing for the favor of the best dancers among the village misses.

The music for such affairs usually is furnished by the men themselves. Some of the camp orchestras would match their wares without embarrassment with some of the best professional players outside of camp. These camps usually are made up of men who have brought musical instruments from home, or have saved from their five-dollar monthly allowance to purchase them. Some, however, have been bought by the company with funds made from charging admission to their social functions. In camps which do not boast of so much talent there are "hillbilly" groups that entertain themselves and the men — except those who like to retire early after a tough day making roadbeds or eradicating blister rust tibes. One company in Illinois, with the co-operation of civic organizations in town, presented a show in the town theater and purchased band instruments with the proceeds. Other outfits have smaller bands which function at the lowering of Colors in the evening or participate in civic parades in the community. Practically all the camps have pianos. Some have been donated by friends, some have been lent to the camp, some have been purchased. The government does not furnish funds for such expenditure, but each company operates a canteen for its men who buy candy, cigarets, razor blades, and many other articles. The profits from these canteens are used for such camp improvements. Much camp musical and vocal talent has been used on local radio programs.

But no camp entertainment program is complete without its "stunt nights." To some of them the villagers are invited. To some of them admission is charged, for the financing of future recreational activities. The boxing shows are the most popular events. Some camps have drawn a "gate" of as many as 3000 spectators. One camp, in New England, has paid for an extensive entertainment program from donations from outsiders who attend their sports and social events. The same is true of other camps. Boxing is most popular in the vicinity of Chicago and on the West Coast, because of the impetus given amateur boxing in those sections of the country. There is hardly a camp that does not make use of its recreation hall on certain nights for this sport.

The vaudeville and minstrel shows top the camp entertainment lists for popularity with the men. "Suzannah" and "The Last Round-Up" and "Sweet Adeline," with the C.C.C. variations and accompaniment by the harmonica or the banjo or the mandolin, usually "bring down the roofs." Camp comics, sometimes in blackface, work out their own versions of the "Sambo and the Chicken" story, and camp gymnasts, tumblers, and magicians are headlined as "stupendous and colossal" performers. Often there are prizes of cigarets and candy, donated by the officers or the foresters for the best acts. And sometimes these parties are followed by moving pictures.

Originally, the men had to go into town to see a movie, but now the movies have been brought to the men. Practically all the camps have an opportunity of seeing moving pictures, either of the educational type or of the entertainment variety, at frequent intervals. Both the U. S. Forest Service and the National Park Service maintain movie equipment which they circulate among the camps. This consists, for the most part, of 16mm.-projectors, and the films usually are those depicting features of the forests and the parks or giving instruction in the work the men are engaged in. In the West, the Forest Service operates a "Showboat" service to the camps — movies and lectures on the forests and their care. In other sections, equipment is made available to the

camps and is transported from camp to camp and operated
by C.C.C. projectionists. In some sections of the country,
professional operators have made rounds of the camps, presenting movie "shows" for an admission price. Many of the
companies, however, have purchased their own equipment,
mostly of the 35mm. size that permits the showing of regulation entertainment films. Mae West, Wallace Beery, and
Tom Mix are sure-fire hits with the men. These films usually
are paid for by charging admission of ten or fifteen cents for
the performances. Films are rented or are borrowed from
the many sources from which films may be obtained without
cost. These include many of the federal government departments and state governments and state universities. Films
also are made available by many industrial organizations.
Government films are mostly of an instructive nature, dealing
with such subjects as soil erosion, plant life, stream pollution,
and forest conservation. The company officers have, in instances, at their own expense, made films of the life and work
in their own camp. In these the men get a chance to see
themselves at work and at play.

There also is a theater "movement" growing in the camps.
Groups are taking up drama seriously. They are studying it
and presenting plays of professional caliber. Comedies,
"mysteries," and "heavy" dramatics hold no terror for some
of the camp players. They attack full-length plays with
the same fearlessness they do one-act pieces. But they
choose, for the most part, those plays which have a minimum
of female characters. The men do, however, take over these
parts when necessary and, occasionally, a young woman from
the community or an officer's wife is drafted into service.
The TERA actors of New York have done much to stimu-
late interest in the theater in the camps of adjoining states.
For a year these troupes have been visiting the camps, presenting some of the more popular plays of the past few years.
Simular groups are working from Chicago and Pacific Coast
cities. These men and women have given their professional
advice and direction to many camp theater organizations.
Stages have been built in one end of many of the recreation

barracks, and ingenuity has been called upon to help with stage scenery and effects. Baking powder cans have been transformed into footlights, and discarded gasoline cans have become flood lights. Scenery has been painted by the men, and more than one camp has an elaborate drop curtain to give its shows a touch of theatrical reality. Some of the men have had experience on the stage, and many of the officers and foresters and educational advisers act as directors and instructors to the classes in the study of drama. Money is raised for scenery and properties by charging an admission fee in the camp or at performances for the community.

C.C.C. men also have become "joiners." No camp is complete without its clubs and societies. The list is a long one. In addition to the groups of Leaders and those others formed for the purpose of camp betterment, there are organizations of various kinds, but mostly social and hobby clubs. Social clubs are formed generally to keep the camp on the "social map" of the C.C.C. They plan and execute social affairs and bring in speakers for lectures and banquets. There are many photography clubs. Hundreds of men have taken up photography as a hobby or to increase their scant supply of money. There is much for the camera in the country in which they are located. Thousands of "snapshots" have been made of the camps and the mountains. These are sent home or sold to other men to be sent home or kept as reminders of their days in the C.C.C. Some of these groups operate their own dark rooms, developing and printing their negatives.

There are mountain-climbing clubs for those men interested in this sport, athletic clubs for the athletes, and forestry clubs for those making forestry a hobby or a profession. Many men are inclined toward "collecting." Stamp collection and the gathering and classifying of arrowheads, insects, flowers, and plants are foremost. The National Park Service and the U. S. Forest Service assist those men interested in forestry and wild life. Their foresters and naturalists act as instructors and guides for many such groups. Some of the men have gone in for a study of animal and bird life and are experimenting in taxidermy.

Interest also is shown in music and singing. There are choral societies and music appreciation groups. Some of the men are of religious bent and many of them take active part in camp church programs or in those of near-by towns. And there are debating clubs which compete, in some instances, with teams of other camps. The short-wave radio furnishes the men a most popular hobby.

There is considerable short-wave radio communication between the camps, handled by the men and, in some of the corps areas, relaying official messages of the C.C.C. The Ninth Corps area early was faced with the problem of communicating with its far-flung district headquarters — stretching from Canada to the Mexican border — and made use of several of the thousands of amateur operators who are members of the Army Amateur Radio system. They enrolled these men and installed equipment for them. The Third Corps area, comprising the states of Pennsylvania, Maryland, and Virginia and the District of Columbia, followed suit. There are thirty stations in this network, and the men are permitted to shift to the amateur wave lengths at night for the handling of free messages for enrollees. Other corps areas already are beginning to make use of the short-wave radio. Independent of these official stations, however, hundreds of dyed-in-the-wool radio "hams," as amateurs are called, have brought their radio knowledge and equipment into camp. Officers and foresters are numbered in this group. They have set up their stations and have provided a channel of communication between many of the men in the camps and their homes. Numerous radio clubs and classes have added to the interest being manifested in this very practical hobby.

Perhaps one of the most extensive schools of journalism has developed in the camps. There are but few outfits that do not have a camp "paper" of some sort. The format of some is that of the tabloid newspaper; of others, that of the humor magazine. Each has its distinctive "masthead," such as: "The District News," or "The Death Valley Echo," or "The Green Guidon," or "The Goldbrick Gossip," or "The Chatterbox." Some of these newspapers are press printed, and of from four to eight pages, but the majority of them are printed by mimeograph. They carry the news of the camp, or of the district, which comprises several camps. Each has its staff of editors, artists, and reporters, and some of them have their own typesetters and pressmen. A few of the camps have secured small presses and type of their own. Here the men get an opportunity of writing their stories, putting them into type, and printing the papers. Some camps cooperate with local newspaper plants that print their newssheets. These papers appear weekly, monthly, bimonthly, or, sometimes, "whenever we have enough news." There is one camp "daily." It is mimeographed and of two pages. Generally those men who work on the papers are those interested in journalism or in writing. Usually they are formed into a group that studies journalism and uses the camp paper as its "laboratory."

A professional newspaper is published in Washington for all the camps. It has the appropriate title: "Happy Days." It keeps the camps informed of what other camps of the country are doing and furnishes them with official news as it originates at the Washington headquarters of Emergency Conservation Work. News from the individual camps is furnished by members of the C.C.C. Press Association, an organization of camp reporters. Many excellent writers and artists are developing in the forest camps, and some of them already have secured employment on the staffs of newspapers and magazines outside of camp. The drawings of this book were done by a C.C.C. man, who was enrolled in New York and spent his maximum time in camps of Montana, Florida, and Tennessee.

Athletics, naturally, play a large part in the recreational life of the camps. Baseball is the most popular. On Saturdays and Sundays the men will crowd into a truck and travel over the mountains or the plains to match their baseball team with that of another camp or a semi-professional team of some one of the surrounding towns. No college or big league team ever got more loyal support from its "backers" than some of these camp teams get. And many of the "top-notch" teams of the country have been forced to bow to the prowess of a C.C.C. pitcher. Several of these players have been offered a "tryout" with teams of the professional baseball leagues. Some of the camps have been matched in competitive play, others have competed in municipal leagues. A nation-wide competition for C.C.C. baseball teams now is being planned. Football and basketball also find many followers. Recreation halls have, in some camps, been made into satisfactory courts for basketball. Camp teams have been given the use of near-by high school and armory floors for their games. Competition in this sport has become highly organized in some of the districts. Ping-pong is the most popular of the "minor" sports, along with the pitching of horseshoes.

Many play chess, checkers, and card games. Gambling, however, is one of the camp "don'ts."

Such is the recreational life of the C.C.C. camp. But for those men who wish to devote a portion of their hours not at work to other things, an educational program is provided. And more than half the men in the camps are so inclined. In many respects, the "School of the Woods" is one of the most significant experiments ever made in education.

HOME WORK

★ 8 ★

THE SCHOOL OF THE WOODS

THE C.C.C. was begun as an experiment in conservation and rehabilitation. The educational program which has grown up in the C.C.C. camps, likewise, is an experiment. Perhaps it will be of some importance to pedagogy. It justly may lay claim, nevertheless, to being one of the largest and, at the same time, most unorthodox of schools. It has approximately 150,000 men in its student body, its classes meet in thousands of buildings, and it is located in every state of the nation. There are no entrance requirements, no definite curriculum is adhered to, and students attend, or not, as they wish.

Young conservationists who make up this School of the Forests are not of common educational background. Some have attended, for a few weeks, or months, mountain schools conducted by church organizations; some have had a few years in public schools. About half have attended high school, some of them having graduated. A small percentage have been in college and, here and there, are some who have college degrees.

To devise an educational program that would offer the greatest opportunity to so widely diversified a group, was the aim of those in charge of Emergency Conservation Work. To return men to their homes better qualified to compete in economic life and with greater understanding of themselves and their relationship to the things and people who make up the world around them, was the object behind the plan of the President and Director Fechner for education in the camps.

Such a program, it was recognized, would need to be built specifically to accomplish this purpose. The men in the camps had become adults, with problems to solve. They could not be "sent to school" like children, who have little concern in or knowledge of the difficulties of life. They had come into intimate contact with matters such as those relating to money, people, and a changing world. Many had left school, either because they had rebelled against it or because family finances were low, and had gone to work. Some of them, before they were forced out by the depression, had found themselves in "blind alley" jobs that promised little. They realized their need of greater education, but thought themselves too old to go back to school. Others had capacity and desire for learning, but had been given neither opportunity nor encouragement at home. Many never had such a desire stirred in them. Either they could not read or write or their education was most meager. Study for them would be embarrassing. It would be a mark of inferiority, and thus a jar to the ego.

Education for such a group of men, it was decided, should relate itself to the interests of the men and become a part of the work, and be interwoven with the life they were living in the forests or intending to follow after leaving camp. It was to this end that plans were made in the fall of 1933 to expand and enlarge and unify the school program which, in one form or another, had been worked out in the individual camps. The War Department was made responsible for education in the camps. It had been one of the features of the C.C.C. welfare program from the beginning, but had not been developed fully because of the lack of trained personnel to direct it. Libraries had been installed, but few of their books were of an educational nature. The men had been encouraged to study, however, and some company commanders had taken considerable interest in this phase of camp life. To bring about uniformity, and to add to the opportunities of education for the men, Director Fechner asked the Department of Education to act in an advisory capacity to the Army.

An extensive advisory set-up was created, headed by a director of C.C.C. education in Washington, who, with an advising group, recommended educational objectives and general means of execution to the War Department. Likewise, as Army responsibility had been delegated to corps area commanders, an adviser was named for each of the corps areas to co-ordinate the work in the areas, under supervisory control of the Army. Their job was that of organizing programs for each corps area consistent with the conditions in each area and in line with the educational policies determined in Washington. In addition, educational advisers were named, one each, for about three fourths of the camps.

There are 1267 such camp advisers. Some work with two or more companies when their camps are adjacent or near each other. The men chosen for these positions were young men, with college training, but not bound by a system of pedagogy that would not lend itself to change. Flexibility was needed in the camp programs. Instruction had to be adapted to the men; the men could not be bent to match a method of teaching. These camp advisers were to become a new sort of teacher. They were to do more than assign lessons in a book and hold students to recitation and examination. They were to seek out the educational interests of their prospective students, and build their program around them. They were to become acquainted with the ambitions and the problems of their men and endeavor to create opportunities for such study as the men wanted and thought would be helpful. They had to do more than try to "sell" education on the sales talk that "education is great stuff, and you should want some of it." Too many of the boys in camp had left school because it had been presented to them in much that manner.

Education had to be made a part of a man's life, through his interests. Thus, if an enrollee wanted to learn about motors, he should be given what opportunities were possible to study mechanics. The man, then, most likely, would feel the necessity of knowing something of mathematics or mechanical drawing or physics. Such education would be meaningful, then, to such a man. There would be a motive for studying. If a man was interested in typing and shorthand and he was given a chance to develop that interest, he would soon discover the value of spelling, and possibly composition. If he wanted to be a farmer, a carpenter, or a business man,

it would not be difficult to lead him into the study of that
which would assist him in becoming a farmer or carpenter
or business man. Writing his name might be made interesting for an illiterate, not by holding him up to embarrassment or ridicule, but by arousing a motive for learning to write,
such as signing the payroll each month, or writing letters home.
The same kind of persuasion might instill in him a desire to
know how to read.

The adviser had to learn early that he was dealing with
adults, some of them locally enrolled men, forty or fifty years
old.   Neither they, nor the young men who had become too old
for grammar school, could be taught like children. He had
to discover motives for education, and, if they were not cul-
tivated, to make an attempt to arouse them. Many of the
young men had no definite idea of what sort of work they
wanted to enter when they left camp, even if it were available. The educational program suggested the enlightenment
of men on various vocations and professions if possible. The
adviser was to discover possible talents and interests of these
men and attempt to direct them toward vocations calling for
such talents and interests. If, for instance, an enrollee's
work in landscaping the company street was marked, and
that man needed vocational guidance, landscaping as a vocation might be suggested to him. Books dealing with the subject would be afforded him and he would be given more opportunity of working at landscaping while in camp. Or, perhaps,
a man displayed ability in drawing. Assisting him in the study
of drawing, advising him on the possibilities of making drawing
his profession, would be the service of the adviser to this man.
Education presented in guise of this kind became something
real and alive to the men — something they wanted, instead
of something they thought was being thrust upon them. Some
of the advisers sent into the camps have done excellent work;
some have not.

·Discovering where the interests and needs of the men lay
was but one phase of the work delegated to camp advisers by
company commanders. As important as knowing what the
men were interested in, was the work of providing them with

facilities of education. Formal classroom instruction would
do for some of the men, but teachers would be required. For
the teaching of motor mechanics or any of the trades, some
sort of laboratory work was essential. For men wishing
more advanced education, equipment and instruction not available within the camp was necessary. The adviser was generally the person who had to provide them. A comparatively
small amount of money was allotted for the purchase of equipment or books, but equipment and books became essential.
So did experienced and competent instructors. To obtain
them, company commanders and educational advisers drew
upon the officers and foresters in the camp who could assist the
men in their study of such things as forestry, road building,
and those trades represented in the work of the camp. Many
of the Reserve Corps officers were college graduates and were
competent to instruct the men in various specified subjects.
They were the first to be called to the faculty of the camp
school.

It was necessary to go into the towns and cities surrounding
the camps for equipment or facilities essential to the growth
of the program. High schools and colleges and universities
were made interested in the educational work in the camps and
urged to participate. Consequently, hundreds of such institutions were brought into the camp educational program.
Many of them opened their doors to the men from the camps
at night, allowing them admission to their own evening ses-
sions, or setting up a program to match their needs and furnishing necessary instructors. Other colleges and universities have sent instructors into the camps. The extension
courses of these institutions also have given freely of their
services to the C.C.C. men. Leaders in various professions
and vocations have been brought into the camps to lecture,
giving the men an insight into law, medicine, mechanics, journalism, insurance, engineering, bee keeping, and poultry raising. Books have been bought and have been donated. Some
of the camps have accumulated educational libraries of several hundred textbooks. One California library numbers
nearly 3,000 volumes. Correspondence courses are used ex-

tensively in most of the camps. One corps area prepares its
own courses.

The majority of the men have expressed interest in vocational study. Their job in the future is of vital interest to them. They have experienced the distress of unemployment and welcome the opportunity of better preparing themselves for employment when they go back home. They are willing to spend their evening hours or part of their week-end free time attending classes in auto mechanics, carpentry, stone masonry, or forestry. Scores of village and town garages have become classrooms for C.C.C. men studying the gasoline motor. Some camps have acquired old automobiles as laboratory equipment for the same purpose. The camp itself offers the men an opportunity of studying at the trades. Camp technical foremen have become instructors as well as work bosses, during the day, and often meet with interested men at night to add to their knowledge of the trades in which they are concerned and to suggest other means of self-education for the men.

Camp work also affords vocational instruction in truck driving, road building, tool making, blacksmithing, and heavy machinery operation. Bookkeeping, typing, stenography, commercial art, electrical engineering, fruit growing, landscape architecture, photography, surveying, dramatics, and cabinet making are among the more popular subjects of study. Through combining work and instruction, enrollees are gaining a knowledge of bridge building, concrete work, irrigation, floriculture, nursery work, telephone line construction, lumbering, log and timber creosoting, tree surgery, warehousing, refrigeration, cooking, and moving picture machine operation.

But vocational interests are not the only concern of the men. Nearly half of the men enrolled in the School of the Forests are delving into cultural subjects, from literature and philosophy to a study of foreign languages, including Latin — even Chinese. Small groups of the men generally are concerned with these courses, usually directed by the educational adviser or a company officer or forester, himself interested in the same subject. Many Reserve Officers of the Army Engineer Corps are on duty with C.C.C. companies. Nearly all of them have become instructors in mathematics to men of their outfits who have expressed a desire to study algebra, geometry, trigonometry, or calculus. Aviation has become a well-attended course in camps where one or more of the officers are of the Air Corps. Navigation and ship management are popular in several camps. One such camp, in Illinois, has its own recruit ship, on a near-by lake, as its "laboratory" of navigation. Another camp has developed instruction in the operation of gliders, and has built a glider field.

Lectures and the variety of classroom instruction common to the prevailing school and college practice are resorted to as little as possible in the camps. It has been supplanted by the discussion group method. And it is this form of study and instruction that has proved most popular and most beneficial. Especially is this true of the "classes" in the study of government and current problems of economics and politics, and the discussion of such questions as marriage and a man's relationship to his family and his country. The men come to many of these group meetings armed with information and comment from books and magazines and newspapers and stand toe to toe with others who express contrary views, generally backed up by information from similar sources. Usually, the adviser or an officer acts as leader of the group, to keep the men to the subject matter of the particular meeting. Sometimes, however, some of the men themselves act as leaders of discussion, and rule with all the authority vested in them.

Developing and furthering interesting leisure time activities also has become a part of the camp educational program. The development of hobbies is encouraged and much assistance is given those men who become interested. Field trips are arranged for collectors of stone, wood, and flower specimens; and textbooks on the drama, stamp collecting, leathercraft, woodcraft, and metalcraft are provided, and materials for the practice of these crafts are purchased in quantities from funds provided by the men. Handicraft, in leather, wood, and the metals, has nearly reached the stage of a vocation with men in many of the camps, particularly those of New England, Michigan, and the Fourth corps area — comprising the states of the Southeast. Leather handbags, belts, and valises made by the men are being sold by them at considerable profit. Woodworking is more popular in the Fourth corps area camps. Tables, chairs, and bedsteads and inlaid trays of walnut are among their most profitable bits of work. Most of this furniture is of true Georgian and Carolinian colonial style.

The aim of the educational program in the C.C.C. camps is that of developing in each man his powers of self-expression, self-culture, and self-entertainment; developing pride and satisfaction in co-operative endeavor; developing an understanding of the economic and social world in which he lives; preserving and strengthening good habits of health and of mental development; affording vocational counseling and opportunities for better equipping the men to secure and hold a job after they leave the forests; developing an appreciation of nature and country life. Its method is that of affording a chance of instruction and study based upon the needs and wishes of the men; of fitting into the life of the men rather than attempting to dictate their lives. That it is succeeding in some of its phases is, of course, indisputable. Thousands of men have and will go back into their usual pursuits with a better understanding of themselves, of their jobs, of the things and the people in the world around them, and with a sharpened realization of their relationships and responsibilities in society. Whether it is making the most of the opportunity it has, becoming a potent influence in the lives of hundreds of thousands of young men of the country, can be determined best by an examination into the future lives of the "graduates" of this "School of the Forests."

That a large number of the men in the C.C.C. are interested in education is evinced by their growing participation in the camp program. Many of the camps have organized their "school' extensively. They have given college and university titles to their officers and foresters and educational advisers. The company commander generally is termed the president of

the Camp "so-and-so" University, or College. One district
of ten companies is so organized — The University of Skokie
Valley. Each company has been designated as a college of
the university. The district commander is the "president,"
and each of the company commanders is "dean" of his college.
The colleges have been given titles after various presidents of
the country. The district chaplain is "dean of men," the district surgeon the "dean" of "The College of Medicine," and a
Student Council is organized for the purpose of increasing the
interest of the men in educational opportunities of the camp.

"Rainy Day" schedules have been adopted at several camps:
when it rains and there is no work, men are afforded lectures
and educational moving pictures. Movies are utilized in many
camps for the furthering of educational activities. One outfit has a large class in parental education, the men discussing
the economic and social problems of marriage and the rearing
of children. The study of state history has been found popular and that of Negro literature is making headway in many
camps of Negroes. A group of men desirous of perfecting
their Spanish occupy a table by themselves in the mess hall
of another camp, and converse entirely in that language during their meals. Sociology and economics find much favor
among the men when they are presented in terms of "jobs and
families." Thousands of these C.C.C. students travel from
five to fifty miles in trucks two or three nights a week to attend school in surrounding towns. A fifty-year-old man in a
Maine camp has begun the study of Latin.

Many of the educational advisers and company officers have
taken upon themselves the task of locating employment for
men of their camps who show marked ability in some definite
field. Graduation exercises are held in nearly all of the camps
for men completing their school work. Education in the C.C.C.
is voluntary. No one has to submit himself to "schooling"
unless he wants to, except to that which pertains to his work
or to camp sanitation or to camp and personal safety. But,
as one enrollee said; "It's fun studying algebra when you don't
have to."

FIGHT NIGHT   100   "COMIN' HOME"

★ *9* ★

GREENER HORIZONS

MEN are working, and playing, in the C.C.C. — and are growing a year or more older. Some are coming out of the woods glad that their enrollment time is up and that they are freed of the restraint of discipline. On nearly all, however, the mountains and the forests will leave their good mark. None will depart from them untouched. Few are able to put into words just what the outdoors, the living with other men, and the working with nature have done to them. But they feel it. Some have tried to express their reactions to the new lands they have seen, the life they have lived, the forest fires they have fought, the roads they have built, and how it feels to go back to a life of the towns and cities.

From New Jersey to Virginia, to Montana, to California, is the Odyssey of one who speaks from a camp in Death Valley:

"CAMP DIX. Two weeks in a tent city with thousands of men of your own age. The first mess line. The horse-play the rookies have foisted upon them. The 'needle with a hook.' VIRGINIA. Six months among the rolling hills of the Blue Ridge Mountains, working in the pines, eating corn bread and finding out about corn 'likker.' Red mud and rain; crisp cold and snow. Our first Southern winter. Swinging an ax, and learning about brush hooks and what to say when you want to square dance with 'that good-looking blonde.' Southern hospitality. MONTANA. 'The Land of Shining Mountains.' Scenery that must beat the Alps. Green lakes surrounded by Douglas fir; grim, red mountains. 'Vanishing Americans' with their squaws, wrapped in blankets. We help clean up a great national park. We fight our first forest fire. A great four months. CALIFORNIA. In Death Valley, be-

101

low sea level where the thermometer hits 110 with devilish regularity and a thousand imps of torture batter at your brain and blister your skin. Next enlistment somewhere else; perhaps north, south, east, west. But wherever it is, we with a flair for the unusual will find it."

A man sees a mountain, in Maine, and the mountain enthralls him: "Mount Katahdin, with personality distinct of its own. Attempts to storm its rugged fastness are historic. But slowly man has proven himself; he has won the privilege of enjoying the beauty of the 'Court of this Monarch' at pleasure. In the footsteps of early trail-blazers come 200 men to camp at the foot of this 'royal ruler.' The task is attended with sentiment. The experience of marvelling at Katahdin."

The redolence, the spirit, and the romance of the forest come to this man in Upper Michigan: "The pioneer spirit is just realistic enough to bring out the ruggedness in us. Already we have a wilderness fever that is like a drug. The whole thing grows on you and it is hard to break away. If you can think of a lumberjack's life in the North Woods as romantic and adventurous, you can picture the life of the C.C.C. above the Straits. If you want adventure you should live here, under the care of the Army (with discipline partly exempted) and working with the Forest Service."

Nature also speaks to this man in Nevada: "We are coming in contact with nature. We have time to study her laws and mysterious passages. Many of us knew very little of nature's beauty and force until we came into the forests to live with her. Observation only is needed. One of the great things of life is the capacity to observe, appreciate, and understand nature. If the C.C.C. does nothing more than impress upon us the love for nature, it will be a success. When we better realize and understand nature the world will be a better place to live in, and war will be but a dream."

An experience with a storm on Uranus Peak: "We were spending the night in the fire tower. The lookout man had fed us well on Forest Service grub and was singing cowboy ballads in a lusty voice, to the accompaniment of his guitar. Then the storm broke, with a gust of wind that rocked the tower and sang through the guy-wires that held the 40-foot high cube on poles. The tops of the pines swayed and rocked. The veil of rain had jumped several ridges and was pounding on the glass windows. The singing died down to humming. Then came the lightning. A heavy clash, and a cloud of smoke rolled out the stove. The gale tore a huge shutter off and flung it into the forest below. We began to think of a soft spot in the green bed of trees at the base of the cliff below the tower. We sat on the edge of the beds. We felt like mortals, sure enough. The tower rocked and moaned. The lightning blinded while the clouds beat their heads together above us and dinned their thunder into our ears. Why had we left the good old earth? Then the storm rolled off to the south and the lookout man picked up his guitar and said: 'What will it be now, boys—"When the Work's All Done This Fall"?' "

Perhaps it's just the feeling of being "free" that tingles the blood in the veins of many C.C.C. men. This is how one of them described it, in a camp at Humptulip, Washington: "Did you ever live and work in the city, with its canyons of streets, its smoke, its grime, and its noises, and see the sun only part of the time? And then get out where the sky is blue and the grass is green and the birds sing and you can fish and climb to your heart's content? Where you can plunge into a beautiful river at sunrise (and darn near freeze to death), spend the day along the trails or with the pines, and then on weekends hike into the mountains? When you reach the top you can look out over the country, and can see the valleys where there must be another river; you get scratched by the brambles and knock the skin off your shins; you breathe the mountain air and the scent of the flowers at your feet. Gee, ain't it grand! You sit on a rock and dream. Then awaken with a start. It's getting late. You hurry back to camp and drop on your bunk, maybe too tired to want your chow, or too weary to undress. But, it's grand! There are others around you, like yourself — in the C.C.C., getting 30 smackers a month and three square meals a day. And you're free, free, free."

A man gets a week-end leave to go home: "Yes, Sir; I'll be back on Monday morning, and thank you, Sir. . . . Gee, I'm

glad I got that leave; now for home and some real fun. . . .
Will the train never come? . . . Here it is. . . . Yes, Mister,
I'm going home for a little vacation. . . . Work hard? . . .
I'll say we do; built a lot of dams already. . . . Gee, this train
is slow. . . . Ah, there's the old home town. . . . Humm,
didn't see anyone I knew at the station. . . . Oh, well, I'll
walk down Main street. . . . Hello, John; I'll bet you're
glad to see me. . . . I've been gone a long time. . . . Didn't
know it? . . . Yeah. . . . So long. . . . Humph. . . . Hi,
Mary! . . . Stuck up, she is; never even noticed me. . . .
Ah, there's the old homestead. Now for the big surprise.
. . . Hello, Jack; where's Pa and Ma? How's things going?
Fine? That's swell. . . . Things look just as they always
did. Sure swell to be home. . . . Guess I'll call up Virginia.
. . . Not there? . . . Yes, I'll write when I get back to
camp. . . . Well, guess I'll go to bed. . . . No; we see
movies at camp. . . .

"Gee, ten more miles back to camp. . . . There's the
old line of tents. . . . Hey, Jimmy! Spud! How's the
gang? Fine? That's great. . . . Sure did have a good time.
But the old town's deader'n ever. . . . Well, guess I'll wash
up. Must be time for chow. . . . What a glorious feeling!"

Forest fire fighting occupied the time of many men for days
and nights. The fires were the big thrills of the forest — terrible thrills. The big fires were in the West. Here is a
description by a man in one of the California camps: "Mid-
night . . . lights flash on in the barracks . . . 'Everybody Out,
FIRE!' . . . 'Dalton's crew on No. 4 truck!' . . . Sleepy men
mumble their way into clothes. . . . 'Ah, nerts!' . . . Sirens
scream. . . . Men aroused to feverish haste now. . . . 'Wonder where it is?' . . . 'How big is it?' . . . 'Hey, Mac, lend
me your jumper' . . . Men clamber on purring trucks. . . .
'Johnson!' . . . 'Here!' . . . 'Butler!' . . . 'Here!' . . . He-
roes of the night . . . to the rescue . . . while the populace
sleeps. . . . Silhouette of trucks with denim-clad men against
looming timber ahead . . . symbolic of Nation's youth. . . .
At the helm. . . . Trucks round the curves. . . . The smoke
. . . then the fire . . . axes . . . shovels . . . backfire trails.

. . . 'Head her off at the point.' . . . Damn. . . . Jumped the backfire. . . . Scramble through brush in frantic haste . . . chopping . . . scraping . . . hacking . . . spraying . . . beating . . . patrolling. . . . Hours . . . Weary crews pile into trucks . . . back to camp. . . . Showers. . . . Sleep."

But this is a different picture, from a camp at Ruch, Oregon, during one of the bad fires that hit that part of the country last summer: "Down the steep hill from the fire as the stars come out of nowhere into the night; weary, dirty, and cinder-covered, after 26 long, work-filled hours on the fire line. We throw ourselves down at the camp fire with the others, some from our camp, some strangers, but all just fire fighters. Someone ventures: 'Had anything to eat?' 'No, can we get anything?' 'Yeh, over there. Tired?' 'Yeh.' Mel and I, last ones down because we were on the high side. Drag our bodies to the cabin where the cooks and K.P.'s are bumping each other in an effort to feed the men as they come in. The cabin, of logs, belongs to a miner who has turned it over to the men as a field kitchen. It is seven o'clock. We have not eaten since breakfast. Everything smells good, and the stove fills the cabin with warmth. Pork and beans and 'corn-willy,' with a sandwich of butter and jam and real coffee. It tastes good and we fill our plates again, and drink more coffee. Then we go back to the camp fire, and lie down. No extra clothes: in the way on the fireline. I listen to the conversation and bet Mel they are from Chicago. 'Sure, I've flown a plane. My brother and I had a little Waco last year.' . . . 'Me? — Naw, fer gosh sakes, she's blonde.' . . . 'Tommy said the fellow who lives here set the fire accidently, burning brush — wanted to shoot himself.' . . . 'Do you first-aid men give the new men their shots?' . . . 'You would laugh, you hypomaniacs' . . . 'Fought it with his hands — crazy.' . . . 'Oh, for a bed.' . . . I begin to feel cold. My side and arm are sore where I've been lying on the ground. The fire has died low. I must have been sleeping. . . . Mel is awake, too. And several others. 'Sleep any, Mel?' 'Yeh, about half asleep.' 'Wonder if we could get some more coffee?' The cooks are still working, making sandwiches to send out to the line. It's about two o'clock.   The sandwiches won't reach them before morning.   Not even a pack mule can get over those shale trails.   There is hot coffee on the stove.   We drink from tin cups.   They make us some more jam and butter sandwiches. We sit on the edge of the miner's bunk and eat them.   It is nice and warm in here, and we roll a cigaret.   My head drops down and I jerk it up.   Then we go out into the air again. We stand with our backs to the camp fire once more.   I lie down again but it's too cold.   I come back to the fire, where I sprawl out.   Oh, Lord, but it's cold.   Then morning comes. The first-aid man and I go down to the creek and wash our faces.   My mouth is dry and thick with too many cigarets. They are talking around the camp fire: — 'Say, wasn't that a hell of a place on that south hill?' . . .   'Nick estimates the area about 1,000 acres.' . . .   'Wonder how soon we'll have to go back?' . . .   'Gosh, I hate to think of going up that hill again.' . . .   Then the cooks call: 'Come and get it.' "

Listen to one of the several thousands of war veterans in the C.C.C.: "To me the C.C.C. is practically the same as the outfit was in the World War.   The only difference is, that in the C.C.C. we handle an ax, while in the war we had a gun.   To-day we find the same class of men we did then.   All hit by the depression.   In the war we spent a lot of time digging trenches and training; now we clean brush, build roads, and make fire trails to better forest land.   Many of the men left good jobs and real positions to go into the war.   Today they have no jobs and had to go into the C.C.C.   I've palled with men who were agents, bank clerks, machinists, ball players, and laborers, all here in camp working in the forests.   I have seen Red chopping down trees.   He was a boiler maker, strong and with the heart of a lion.   I have watched Mac plowing up the road.   Once he was one of the best publicity men on the West Coast.   A smart man, with lots of experience.   I have seen Sam building fires for the laundry.   Sam is a crooner, and a professional actor, as good as you can find on any stage. They're all here, and doing a real job of work.   We have made over a congested ravine of tangled underbrush, weeds, and red-wood into a little village.   You can imagine how we felt, after traveling over the mountains, to find such a site for our camp, and then watch it grow into the place it is now. If you chance up Annapolis way, up the coast from San Francisco, stop by. You'll see some real work done in the forests, and a campful of real men."

Now from Ottine, Texas. By a boy who was a "softie": "When people used to call me a 'softie,' it was true. I was mother's pet. Just a kid who was sickly all his days, and whose mother would not push him out into the world to fight for himself. Petted, pampered, and given nearly everything that I desired, I became selfish, uncourageous; I was like a 'jellyfish.' I was taking life easy, and expecting it always to be that way — until the time came when there wasn't any more money to keep the home comforts going. I then joined the C.C.C. One of the first things I learned was that it took money to buy food and clothes, as well as luxuries. Then I learned what it means to work, not just drift. I am still a rookie, but I have a job, and something to do, and I am learning to take a pride in the work I do. There must be many other boys who were 'softies,' and who will say with me, 'thanks for the C.C.C. and the chance it has given us.' "

That from a "rookie." Now this from a Missouri man who has served his time in the C.C.C.: "We, the old men of the C.C.C., who have seen a year of service in the organization, soon are to leave. And we give to the rookies the challenge to carry on as we have. We were given a new, untried work to do, and we have done it. Now we give the new men a perfected organization, to do with as they will. We dare them to do their best, to build it yet higher, better, more efficient in its operation. Take the banner we received from the President so gladly, and carry it higher, more boldly than we. We have done our best; do the same, you rookies. Blaze new roads in this adventure of economic rehabilitation."

The spirit which has grown up in the camps is akin to that which permeates a college or university, yet is of a more profound nature. A boy from Nevada City camp says this: "The Spirit of the C.C.C. is a difficult thing to describe, because it, like the organization itself, is something new. The country was full of unemployed men — forgotten men. The Civilian Conservation Corps was organized — so sudden and miraculously that it is almost indescribable. The spirit of the C.C.C. is based upon the sympathetic and overwhelming desire to assist in relieving a depression. It is continually pumping from the arteries of the men who know no defeat. Each one of us seems to be bubbling over with excess vitality and a keen desire to push the Corps to success. It is the spirit of the Revolutionary days; the spirit behind Abraham Lincoln."

Another has this to say: "And so I became a C.C.C. member. 'Six months to be wasted,' they said when I left. But, no! I'm finding a world of knowledge. Knowledge I'll never get in college. One side of my education, of which I only had a glimpse, is just beginning. Yesterday, I started to push against a tall snag. My foreman warned me away. Told me once he had pulled a dead man out from under such a snag. He had done what I had started to do, and had been killed by the falling of the rotten wood and bark. I have learned to tell the hemlock from the spruce, and the pine from the fir. I can blaze a trail and know what to look for at a corner section. Last night I helped the surveyor. Now I know what latitude and departure are. And when they speak of a traverse, I understand. I had to ask what 'widow makers' are, and it took me three days to learn the meaning of a 'highballer' and the 'goldbricker.' Today I can sharpen an ax. Last month I would have ruined one. Yes, and I have learned to 'take it.' I can laugh now — even if I get thrown into the 'crick' or find some crawly thing in my bunk. The list of things I have learned is long, and grows longer each day. I glory in each new bit of knowledge and look forward to what the morrow will bring. No, not six months of wasted time."

Here is a farewell thought of a Pennsylvania man who has been in the camps for his limit: "Outside my window the snow is softly drifting down in feathery-white clouds, covering the bleak landscape with a beautiful whiteness. Through its haze I can dimly glimpse the background of the near-by mountains, those wooded hills whose beauty has never ceased to impress me with their magnificence. It brings back memories of that day which, if judged by time, means nothing, a mere interlude, but if judged by the wealth of experience, and the gain in mental and physical attributes, a lifetime, that day when we first viewed this camp of ours. We were new to the game then, wondering what the future held in store for us — if we would be able to stick it out — or, as we learned to call it afterwards, 'take it.' Little did we realize then that there was untold happiness awaiting us in this first forest refuge, away from the artificial pleasures of the city. Troubles, yes — we are never immune to them, whether in the midst of a maddening throng or in a quiet, sylvan hide-away. But the greatest troubles for us were ended — starvation, want, suffering. And so, with our biggest problems solved, we were better able to cope with the small ones. We were determined to do our best. Some of us failed — attribute that to human frailty. But the rest of us proved that we could 'take it,' and in the proving increased our ability to stand on our own feet, to solve our own problems, and eventually to come out on top. There may be some people who will say, 'You'll have to stick it out, there's no other choice.' Perhaps they are right, but what of it? We shall all cherish the memory of this brief adventure. We shall be proud to have been pioneers, as we are proud of our forefathers. We say farewell with regret, but face the future with enthusiasm, feeling that we have proven ourselves men."

And now for a C.C.C. valedictory: "Into the chaotic conditions caused by the last great world conflict have come the courageous youth of our country, the innocent victims of conditions in which they had no part and over which they had no control. Without bitterness at their lot, but with true nobility, and with courage, faith, and hope they have accepted the challenge of adversity and are humbly beginning new steps in the slow, arduous climb back to normal human activities. They have gone forth to conserve the forests, soils, and watersheds which have been God's gift of natural resources to the United States. It is a conservation of youth, its morale and self-respect. America, we thank you for this opportunity to serve you. America, our gift to you is the consecration of our lives, our minds, and our efforts to your best interests."

NO "GOLDBRICKING" HERE

* 10 *

"NATIONAL RESOURCES"

MAN cannot live apart from Nature. The relationship is closer, perhaps, than man in his egocentricity has been forced to admit. But when man is touched by want, the satisfaction of which lies in Nature, he is "brought to earth," not figuratively, but quite actually. If he has to abandon his farm because the rain has washed off the top soil and crops will not grow, he may curse the land, load the family into the car, and move into town. But if he finds the town already overcrowded, and no job to be had, he may have to sell the car to buy food. Then, if he is a wise man, he will realize that he should have done something to prevent the rain washing the top soil from his farm. Another of the men touched by want may have earned his livelihood in the forests, and have been burned out of a job. Another may have seen his farm covered with red clay washed down over it by a swollen adjacent stream from the watershed miles away. And another may have lived in the city and have lost home and family when a flooded river surged over its banks. Such disasters turn our thoughts to Nature, and from them we may gain an understanding of our dependence on it.

Apparently the economic strife of the past few years has brought a large number of men "to earth"; — at least, men are becoming conscious of the part that Nature does play in their schemes of livelihood. Droughts and wind storms that bury farm land under a foot or more of sand, floods that ravish and kill, forest fires that burn men out of possible jobs, have helped to make both the farmer and the city man, who buys meat and wheat at higher prices, wonder what should be done about it. Some men see, too, that this is but one phase of

Nature; one facet of the relationship that exists between them and the natural resources which feed their wants.

"In recent years," President Roosevelt said in a message to Congress, "little groups of earnest men and women have told us of this havoc, of the cutting of our last stands of virgin timber, of the increasing floods, of the washing away of millions of acres of our top soils, of the lowering of our water table, of the dangers of one-crop farming, of the depletion of our minerals — in short the evils we have brought upon ourselves today and the even greater evils that will attend our children unless we act."

He also mentioned the element of relationship between Man and Nature. He said: "Man and nature must work hand in hand. The throwing out of balance of the resources of nature throws out of balance also the lives of men. We find millions of our citizens in villages and on the farms — stranded there because nature cannot support them in the livelihood they had sought to gain through her. We find other millions gravitated to centers of population so vast that the laws of natural economics have broken down. If the misuse of our natural resources alone were concerned, we should consider our problem only in terms of land and water. It is because misuse extends to what men and women are doing with their occupations and to their many mistakes in herding themselves together that I have chosen to use the broader term, 'national resources.' "

The Civilian Conservation Corps, the work it has done in conserving natural resources, and the rehabilitation which has taken place in its ranks — giving hundreds of thousands of men jobs, re-creating their morale, assisting financially their families at home and giving them the advantage of experience in a life of work and play and associations — significantly illustrates the "national resources" expressed by the President. In fact, the ideals behind Emergency Conservation Work patently sprang from the same fountain source. And while its accomplishments, in so short a time, might not afford a precise exemplification of the possibilities in a more extensive program of similar design, it might be used as a quadrant.

An evaluation of the C.C.C. could begin with the benefits derived personally by the men, but it also would need to count in those accruing to their families, to the participating departments of government, to the many acres of land saved from erosion, to the parks of the nation and the states, and to the forests. When the first 250,000 young men were sent into the forest lands to work, there was considerable question among those veterans of many forest fires and many years of toil trying to hold the forests to their own, as to the possible good that might be accomplished, other than giving the men a place in which to live and have a few dollars in their pockets. But the technical services co-operating in Emergency Conservation Work have been responsible for teaching hundreds of thousands of these men to work, and camp superintendents and foremen have been much more to them than "bosses" — they have been teachers, counselors, and co-workers. The Department of Agriculture and the Department of the Interior have planned the work to be done and carried through their part of the C.C.C. program with real understanding of the problem of both conservation and rehabilitation.

Whether a greater amount of work, or more efficient work, could have been purchased with the money which went to pay for the keep and the allowances to the men of the C.C.C. does not matter much. What is significant, however, is that very few of the old-time foresters have failed to sound their praise of the work the C.C.C. men have turned in each month they have been in the forests. Many thousands of miles of fire trail and break have been completed that might never have been there if there had been no C.C.C. Many, many acres of forests still are living that might now have been burned if the C.C.C. men had not responded as they did to their training as forest-fire fighters. Insects and disease have been eradicated or controlled in hundreds of thousands of acres of timber land, or parks, which might still be choking elms and oaks and pines but for the work of the crews in blue denim. The past year was one of the worst ever in its fire hazard, yet the loss from fire in the forests was reduced tremendously. Our national parks give evidence of the work the men have accomplished in them, and the many new state parks which now are developing indicate that Emergency Conservation Work has at least been an incentive to furthering state consciousness of the possibilities of doing something with their forest lands.

The men have not been worked hard in most of the camps. In some few the "going" has been tough, because of the nature of the job at hand or because of the nature of the superintendent in charge. The C.C.C. may not have accomplished as much in the time they have been in the camps as experienced hands would have done, but the fact that there is a persistently increasing demand from forestry officials that a permanent conservation group, such as the C.C.C., be maintained in the woods is convincing testimony in behalf of the men from the cities. The value of the work the men have done, at the last accounting, has been placed at $291,000,000.

The U. S. Army has played an important role in its control of the men in the camps, their transportation, their feeding, their clothing, their shelter, their pay. It has been the largest peacetime operation the Army has performed, — and not without benefit to the Army. Thousands of Reserve Corps officers have been afforded an opportunity of working with men "in the field." There has been no drilling, no target practice, no battle charge to lead, but there have been problems of discipline which are quite as much the part of an officer's training as is that of commanding men under fire. Because the disciplinary measures at the disposal of the officer were less stringent than those of the Army, these officers have been called upon in many instances to display leadership and ability to command in excess of that normally required with more "power" behind them. The Army has had an opportunity of testing its decentralized system of responsibility while working under conditions as near those of real warfare as possible during times of peace. The enrollment, conditioning, transporting, and clothing of the men has been an experience almost tantamount to that of recruiting troops for war. The equipping and supplying the C.C.C. companies in the field has paralleled that necessary for troops awaiting action, and in some respects more difficult — the outfits located as they are over so wide a territory and some in almost inaccessible reaches of the mountains. Nor has the handling of the funds of Emergency Conservation Work been but "home work" for the finance officers of the Army, or the "policy" problems child's play for the staff officers in charge of C.C.C. activities. And, in addition, and to no small benefit, participation in Emergency Conservation Work has brought the Army in a favorable role before the public, a public largely pacifistic at heart. It has, in some measure, gained approbation from many who looked upon the Army as one with only office-desk generals. The Army has done much for the success of the C.C.C.; it has gained much for itself.

At times such as those attending the organization of the C.C.C., money going into circulation appeared to be of importance as a "prime" for the well of economic prosperity. Nearly half a billion dollars had been put into circulation by the beginning of 1935 through Emergency Conservation Work channels. Of this, more than $143,000,000 had been paid in cash allowances to the men, of which $113,000,000 had been sent directly to the families of the men, and the rest, from $5 to $10 per month, had been paid to the men. The clothing bill for the men reached $50,000,000; shelter cost $30,000,000 more; medical attention, $7,000,000. The remainder went for equipment and in wages to the supervisory and administrative personnel and for feeding the men. All of this money eventually went into the towns and cities of the country and was exchanged for raw materials, for automobile trucks, for shovels, for books and magazines, for radios, and to cigaret makers and candy makers and home-town grocer, butcher, and landlord. There is no definite means of checking on its effectiveness to "turn the tide" from depression. It is known, nevertheless, that individually it marked the measure of difference between being on or off charity lists for the families of no small percentage of the men, and in some instances was the only means of keeping families together.

But what of rehabilitation?

The men who leave the C.C.C. are not rehabilitated. That

implies re-establishment in a former state. No one leaving the C.C.C. ever will be the person he was when he raised his right hand and took the oath to "obey all rules and regulations." No one can spend even six months in a forest camp and not be affected by it. Some, to be sure, have gained or lost more or less than others. Many of the men themselves do not realize what their stay in the mountains or in the forests, under discipline, has done to them. It may be years before they do. But affect them, it has. Being outdoors, in the sunshine, with plenty of exercise and a certain regularity in sleeping has done much for each of them, physically. Under medical care constantly, the men have been afforded much they would not have had access to outside the camp. With few exceptions, they have developed their bodies physically, filling out the underweight ones, and giving strength to muscles. But perhaps the most lasting benefit the men will take home with them, from the standpoint of health, is a knowledge of sanitation, personal hygiene, and first aid, instruction in which has been mandatory in the camps. Hundreds of motorists who have met with accidents near C.C.C. camps will testify to the efficiency of C.C.C. first-aid men. These camp assistant "medicos" have been credited with saving the lives of many such mishap victims. Understanding of the principles of health will stay with the men longer, perhaps, than the weight they put on their bodies.

Too, these young foresters have learned what work is — whether they have learned to like it or not. Under direction of the superintendents and foremen of the technical services, they have had the advantage of working for men who, for the most part, were interested in them personally. The great majority of such supervisory positions are filled by persons of high type, and they have been both inspiration and mentor to thousands of the men who have worked under them. There have been "goldbrickers" among the men, as there are in any group of workers, but, under discipline, even these men learned.

The discipline under which they have lived has given some of the men the most valuable heritage of all. Some had come from homes in which there had been a laxity of control by the parents. Some, also, had been injured by too much parental dictation. Both have benefited from their camp experience. Life in camp also teaches men much of self-discipline. It is an intangible thing which will be of inestimable value. Likewise, the men have gained in knowledge of money — its power, its worth, and the difficulty attending its acquisition at times; also the ease with which it can be spent or lost in gaming. The responsibility which comes to a man in camp is considerable. He must maintain his equipment satisfactorily or must pay for his neglect. He is given authority over others and has the opportunity of learning how to give orders as well as take them. He is away from home, and "on his own." There is responsibility attached to that. And he feels a certain sense of responsibility for the family at home that he is assisting to support with his wages.

One of the lessons which most men have to learn when they grow up and enter the world of affairs is how to get along with other persons. A man gets a measure of this in his own family, but when that is increased to 200 other young men the training is more realistic. Men in the camps naturally must meet this problem, for co-operation in effort is essential to the well-being of both the camp and the individual. In morals, the man will be guided by the same factors that would have guided him or did guide him in his home town. Some of the men will learn "words" that are not of their own vocabulary; they will succumb to the habit of their use as they would have done, had they first heard such words in mill or office.

An opportunity of seeing various parts of the country, which has been given some men through their service in the C.C.C., is of both educational and esthetic value to them. As lasting, perhaps, will be the ideals of conservation of nature and nature's endowments which the men are learning first hand. Few of them will leave the forests without a keener insight into the need of, and the possibilities in, conservation. They will know that man dare not release his efforts to control it without being bested.

Every C.C.C. man has an opportunity of increasing the scope of his education while in camp. More elaborate and complete educational programs have been provided in some camps than in others, depending on the officers in charge, the educational adviser, and the desire of the men for educational work. Much can be done to assist the men educationally during their stay in camps. Many of the enrollees are men who left school because they did not like it. These men can be shown the advantages of a greater understanding of themselves, their fellow-beings, and the world in which they live. Much is being done to acquaint them with various vocations, but facilities for extensive instruction of this sort are limited. Some are learning to read and write; others are preparing themselves for entrance to college.

The C.C.C. is a great school in itself, an "institution," the vast possibilities of which have not been plumbed. The lives of hundreds of thousands of young men of the age when they are most responsive to direction, are gathered together under discipline. They can be taught much, about work, about the government that is making their stay in the forests possible, and about the lives they have to live. Emergency Conservation Work is a "lesson" in government. Driving a four-team hitch that never before had been driven together was the job of Director Fechner when he took over the reins of the largest conservation program ever attempted. He has kept his vehicle out of mudholes and straight on the roads through the forests.

What the future of the C.C.C. will be no one, not even the President, knows, for he does not know how long "the emergency" will last. That it will be continued for another year or more is evident. Whether it will become a permanent agency of government rests with the President and with Congress. Its need seems apparent; its worth demonstrated. At any event, life in the C.C.C. camp is a Great Adventure.